Azure Arc-enabled Data Services Revealed

Deploying Azure Data Services on Any Infrastructure

Second Edition

Ben Weissman
Anthony E. Nocentino
Foreword by Jes Schultz

Apress®

Azure Arc-enabled Data Services Revealed: Deploying Azure Data Services on Any Infrastructure

Ben Weissman
Nürnberg, Bayern, Germany

Anthony E. Nocentino
Oxford, MS, USA

ISBN-13 (pbk): 978-1-4842-8084-3
https://doi.org/10.1007/978-1-4842-8085-0

ISBN-13 (electronic): 978-1-4842-8085-0

Managing Director, Apress Media LLC: Welmoed Spahr
Acquisitions Editor: Jonathan Gennick
Development Editor: Laura Berendson
Coordinating Editor: Jill Balzano

Cover image designed by Freepik (www.freepik.com)

Distributed to the book trade worldwide by Springer Science+Business Media LLC, 1 New York Plaza, Suite 4600, New York, NY 10004. Phone 1-800-SPRINGER, fax (201) 348-4505, e-mail orders-ny@springer-sbm.com, or visit www.springeronline.com. Apress Media, LLC is a California LLC and the sole member (owner) is Springer Science + Business Media Finance Inc (SSBM Finance Inc). SSBM Finance Inc is a **Delaware** corporation.

For information on translations, please e-mail booktranslations@springernature.com; for reprint, paperback, or audio rights, please e-mail bookpermissions@springernature.com.

Apress titles may be purchased in bulk for academic, corporate, or promotional use. eBook versions and licenses are also available for most titles. For more information, reference our Print and eBook Bulk Sales web page at http://www.apress.com/bulk-sales.

Any source code or other supplementary material referenced by the author in this book is available to readers on GitHub at https://github.com/Apress/azure-arc-enabled-data-services-revealed-2-edition.

Printed on acid-free paper

To Franzie and Gwendolyn
—Ben

To my family
—Anthony

Table of Contents

About the Authors

Ben Weissman is the owner and founder of Solisyon, a consulting firm based in Germany and focused on business intelligence, business analytics, and data warehousing. He is a Microsoft Data Platform MVP, the first German BimlHero, and has been working with SQL Server since SQL Server 6.5. Ben is also an MCSE, Charter Member of the Microsoft Professional Program for Big Data, Artificial Intelligence, and Data Science, and a Certified Data Vault Data Modeler. If he is not currently working with data, he is probably travelling to explore the world.

Anthony E. Nocentino is a Principal Field Solution Architect at Pure Storage as well as a Pluralsight Author, a Microsoft Data Platform MVP, Linux expert, and corporate problem solver. Anthony designs solutions, deploys the technology, and provides expertise on business system performance, architecture, and security. Anthony has a bachelor's and master's in computer science with research publications in high-performance/low-latency data access algorithms and spatial database systems.

Acknowledgments

Let me start by thanking Franzie – for being the best partner and most amazing mother to me and Gwenny.

Also, thank you to my colleagues at Solisyon for all their hard work that allows me to take the time out for fun projects like this book.

Thank you, Anthony! Not just for yet another joint project but for being an amazing friend!

Dear #sqlfamily: thank you for being who you are. I have never seen a community like ours, and it's an honor to be part of it. There are way too many to call you all out – but you know who you are.

Thank you to the entire Azure Arc-enabled Data Services Team for building an amazing product but especially to Travis, for initially getting me hooked, and to Jes, for taking the time to write our foreword and even more so for always being here for us when we have questions!

—Ben Weissman

First and foremost, I need to thank my wife, Heather. She is my best friend and partner. This year, we celebrate 22 years of marriage together. Every single day with you is better than the previous one. I love you and thank you for all of your unwavering support, inspiration over the years, and listening to me ramble on about tech stuff. I want to thank my two loving daughters, Gabby and Charlotte, for "*SQL Server, SQL Server, SQL Server*," "*Kubernetes is a fancy drink*," and "*Sassy Sausage*." I love you. You are an endless source of joy and pride to me.

Next, thank you to the SQL and Data Platform MVP communities. So many of you have contributed to who I am today as a person and technologist. I want to call out my co-author Ben Weissman, for your vision for this book and friendship; thank you. I am truly lucky to have you as a colleague and friend. I want to also say thanks to my container-mate Andrew Pruski, who is originally from Wales but now based in Ireland. Andrew and I are constantly talking about all things SQL Server, containers, and Kubernetes; thank you for helping review this book. I also want to call out Mark

ACKNOWLEDGMENTS

Wilkinson and Andrew again; we co-organized EightKB this year together, and it was a banging success. That project, your friendship, and our endless ramblings in Slack are what has helped me survive quarantine. Thank you!

To the many friends on the SQL Server Engineering Team that I have made over the last few years, thank you! Jes Schultz, thank you for the fantastic foreword, being a fantastic member of the SQL Server community, and now driving Azure Arc-enabled Data Services forward as the PM. To Bob Ward, for being such an enormous part of the SQL Server community, bringing excellence in engineering and education and teaching the world how SQL Server works under the hood. You truly are an inspiration to me and our community. To Slava Oks, for your excellence in engineering and bringing SQL Server to Linux. It's been a pleasure knowing you and watching your career since we ran into each other years ago in Lisbon. To the whole SQL Server Engineering Team, thank you for your endless technical innovations, engagement in the SQL Server community, and replying to my emails.

To the Apress team, Jonathan, Jill, and Laura, you've truly made this process easy. We couldn't have done this without your support.

—Anthony E. Nocentino

Foreword

When I started my IT career, we ran applications and databases on physical servers. In the first few years, there was a shift to virtualization, and it was a radical transformation with much change. What was a monumental shift then has become commonplace – even the norm – now.

Today, there is another paradigm shift taking place – the move to containerization. I see it in new applications being built by developers eager to have lightweight, repeatable deployments across infrastructures. This is also affecting the world of data, as those developers look to have their containerized applications connect to data sources that are also lightweight and easily deployable.

This shift brings new challenges for the data professional – in a containerized world, with companies rapidly adopting one or more clouds, how do you secure, manage, and monitor data services across these landscapes? Microsoft has been on two parallel journeys for many years – first to bring SQL Server to Linux and containers, and to make Azure SQL Database the best cloud-based operational database in the world. Now, these two roads have been merged with Azure Arc-enabled Data Services, which allow you to run Azure Platform-as-a-Service data services on the Kubernetes distribution of your choice, in the infrastructure of your choice.

I'm excited that two experts have collaborated to bring you this book, designed to get you using Azure Arc-enabled Data Services as quickly as possible. They understand the challenges that come with this new paradigm and break them down into easily understandable chunks of knowledge.

The first time I saw Anthony Nocentino present was at a SQLSaturday in Cleveland, Ohio, in 2020 – the last in-person event I attended before the pandemic. I had been delving into the world of SQL Server on Linux and containers and was interested to hear what he had to say about containers. I was delighted by his deep knowledge and presentation style.

The first time I saw Ben Weissman present was unfortunately online, as an ocean separates us. He was talking about a technology that I have found fascinating since the first time I heard of it – SQL Server Big Data Clusters. Ben had a passion for the technology, making it easy to understand, and was gracious and funny.

With this, I hope you enjoy learning about and working with this technology as much as I do! I can't wait to hear your stories of how you're using Azure Arc-enabled Data Services and how they enable you to do more as an IT professional!

—Jes Schultz

Program Manager, Azure Arc-enabled Data Services

Introduction

When we first started talking about writing a book about Azure Arc-enabled Data Services, the product was in its early private preview stages. We both were very excited about what Azure Arc-enabled Data Services are about to become as a product: This was where all the technology that was recently introduced – like SQL on Linux and SQL on Kubernetes – was coming together. This was the answer to the question why Microsoft did all this.

But, even without that background, we both saw the tremendous value that Azure Arc-enabled Data Services were going to provide. One of the huge challenges that companies have in cloud adoption is being locked in to a vendor's infrastructure. Being locked in to a software is fine – honestly, this has pretty much always been the case from the second you chose a database platform, for example – but infrastructure is a different challenge. You may just not be able or willing to move to the public cloud or may already be invested in some other cloud provider's infrastructure. With Azure Arc, including Azure Arc-enabled Data Services, we were now able to deploy those solutions that previously were exclusively available to Microsoft's Azure Cloud to any cloud on any infrastructure!

It was clear to us that with Azure Arc-enabled Data Services becoming generally available, we just had to keep this book up to date and add all the new features that went into the product since our first edition of this book.

This book introduces you to Azure Arc-enabled Data Services and the powerful capabilities they provide. You'll learn how to benefit from the centralized management that Azure provides, the automated rolling out of patches and updates, and more.

This book is the perfect choice for anyone looking for a hybrid or multi-vendor cloud strategy for their data estate. We will walk you step by step through the possibilities and requirements to get services like Azure SQL Managed Instance or PostgreSQL Hyperscale deployed outside of Azure so they become accessible to companies that either can't move to the cloud or don't want to use the Microsoft cloud exclusively. The technology described in this book will be especially useful to those who are required to keep sensitive services such as medical databases away from the public cloud, but who still want to benefit from the Azure Cloud and the centralized management that it supports.

Book Layout

We split this book into nine separate chapters that will each build on each other to give you a full picture of what Azure Arc-enabled Data Services are:

- Chapter 1, "A Kubernetes Primer": Kubernetes is the architectural backbone of every Azure Arc-enabled Data Services installation. This chapter introduces Kubernetes, describing its role in modern application deployment, the benefits it provides, and its architecture.

- Chapter 2, "Azure Arc-enabled Data Services": This chapter introduces you to Azure Arc-enabled Data Services! We will introduce the core Azure Arc-enabled resources, including servers, Kubernetes, SQL Server, and Data Services. We will then dive deeper into what Azure Arc-enabled Data Services are, its architecture, how workloads are deployed and managed, and discuss key deployment considerations such as compute and storage capacity planning.

- Chapter 3, "Getting Ready for Deployment": In this chapter, we will walk you through the required steps that need to be taken care of before you can start deploying your own Azure Arc-enabled Data Services.

- Chapter 4, "Installing Kubernetes": In this chapter, we will guide you through the setup process of a Kubernetes Cluster, which is required to deploy Azure Arc-enabled Data Services.

- Chapter 5, "Deploying a Data Controller in Indirect Mode": Next, we will guide you on what needs to be done – either using a graphical user interface or the command line – to deploy an Azure Arc-enabled Data Controller within your Kubernetes Cluster that will not be constantly connected to the Azure Cloud.

- Chapter 6, "Deploying a Data Controller in Direct Mode": In this chapter, we will guide you on how to deploy a Data Controller to a Kubernetes Cluster that is connected to the Azure Cloud – and we'll even show you how to deploy this from the Azure Portal.

– Chapter 7, "Deploying an Azure Arc-enabled SQL Managed Instance": With our Data Controller ready and waiting, we can now go ahead and start deploying a first database instance so we can start working with our Arc instance. Similar to the deployment of a Data Controller, we can either use the command line and the azure-cli directly or use a wizard in Azure Data Studio for this.

– Chapter 8, "Deploying Azure Arc-enabled PostgreSQL Hyperscale": While Chapter 7 was handling SQL Managed Instances, this chapter will guide you through the necessary steps when it comes to working with PostgreSQL Hyperscale instead.

– Chapter 9, "Monitoring and Management": In this last chapter, we will focus on how to monitor and manage your Azure Arc-enabled Data Services by leveraging both local management services and Azure's management capabilities.

CHAPTER 1

A Kubernetes Primer

Welcome to *Azure Arc-enabled Data Services Revealed*! This chapter introduces Kubernetes, describing its role in modern application deployment, the benefits it provides, and its architecture. Starting with its benefits, you will learn the value Kubernetes provides in modern container-based application deployment. Next, you will learn how the Kubernetes API enables you to build and deploy next-generation applications and systems in code. In that segment, you will learn the core API primitives Kubernetes provides to define and deploy applications and systems. Then you will learn the key concepts of a Kubernetes Cluster and its components. To finish the chapter off, you will learn the role of Kubernetes in Azure Arc-enabled Data Services.

Introducing Kubernetes

Kubernetes is a container orchestrator. It has the responsibility of starting up container-based applications on servers in a data center. To do this, Kubernetes uses *API Objects* representing resources in a data center, enabling developers and system administrators to define systems in code and use that code to deploy. Container-based applications are deployed as *Pods* into a *Kubernetes Cluster*. A Cluster is a collection of compute resources, either physical or virtual servers, called *Nodes*. Let's dive into each of these elements in more detail, starting with the benefits of Kubernetes and understanding the value it provides in modern application deployment.

1

© Ben Weissman and Anthony E. Nocentino 2022
B. Weissman and A. E. Nocentino, *Azure Arc-enabled Data Services Revealed*,
https://doi.org/10.1007/978-1-4842-8085-0_1

Benefits of Kubernetes

The following are the important benefits that Kubernetes brings to the table:

- **Workload Scheduling**: Kubernetes is a container orchestrator having the primary goal of starting up container-based applications, called Pods, on Nodes in a Cluster. It is Kubernetes' job to find the most appropriate place to run a Pod in the Cluster. When scheduling Pods on Nodes, a primary concern is determining if a Node has enough CPU and memory resources to run the assigned workload.

- **Managing State**: When code is deployed into Kubernetes, defining a workload that needs to be running, Kubernetes has the responsibility to start up Pods and other resources in the Cluster and keep the Cluster in the desired state. If the Cluster's running state skews from the desired state, Kubernetes will try to change the Cluster's running state to get the running state of the Cluster back into the defined desired state. For example, if a Deployment defines having a number of Pods running. If a Pod fails, Kubernetes will deploy a new Pod into the Cluster, replacing the failed Pods, ensuring the number of Pods defined by the Deployment are up and running. Further, suppose you want to scale the number of Pods supporting an application to add more capacity. In that case, you increase the number of replicas in the Deployment, and Kubernetes will create additional Pods in the Cluster ensuring the desired state is realized. More on this in the upcoming section on Controllers.

- **Consistent Deployment**: Deploying applications with code enables repeatable processes. The code defining a Deployment is the configuration artifact and can be placed in source control. You can also use this code to deploy identical systems in down-level environments such as development environments or even between on-premises systems and the cloud. More on this in the upcoming section on the Kubernetes API.

- **Speed**: Kubernetes enables fast, controlled deployments, starting Pods in a Cluster quickly. Furthermore, in Kubernetes, you can scale applications rapidly. Expanding the number of Pods supporting an application can be as simple as changing a line of code, and this can take as little as seconds. This speed is demonstrated in Chapter 6 by adding additional replicas to a PostgreSQL Hyperscale deployment.

- **Infrastructure Abstraction**: The Kubernetes API provides an abstraction or wrapper around the resources available in a Cluster. When deploying applications, there is less focus on infrastructure and more on how applications are defined, deployed, and consume the Cluster's resources. The code used for deployments will describe how the deployment should look, and the Cluster will make that happen. If applications need resources such as public IP addresses or storage, that becomes part of the deployment, and the Cluster will interact with underlying infrastructure to provision these resources for the application's use. This infrastructure abstraction is key to the design and implementation of Azure Arc-enabled Data Services. We will explore this concept more at the end of this chapter.

- **Persistent Service Endpoints**: Kubernetes provides persistent IP and DNS naming for applications deployed in the Cluster. As Pods can come and go due to scaling operations, life cycle operations, or reacting to failure events, Kubernetes provides this persistent networking abstraction for accessing these applications. Depending upon the type of Service used, the Service can load balance application traffic to the Pods supporting the application. As Pods are created and destroyed, based on either scaling operations or in response to life cycle operations or failures in the Cluster, Kubernetes automatically updates the information on which Pods provide the application services.

The Kubernetes API

The Kubernetes API provides a programmatic layer representing the resources available in a data center. The API enables you to write code to consume those resources in your application deployments. When writing code to consume the API, you use *API Objects*, which you use to define and deploy application workloads in Kubernetes.

The code you write is submitted to the *API Server*. The API Server is the core communication hub in a Kubernetes Cluster. It is the primary way you interact with a Kubernetes Cluster and the only way Kubernetes components inside a Cluster exchange information. With the new Cluster state defined, either on initial deployment or by modifying an existing deployment, Kubernetes begins to implement the state described in your code. The desired state of your code becomes the running state in the Cluster.

API Objects

Kubernetes API Objects represent resources available in a Cluster. There are API Objects for compute, storage, and networking elements, among others, available in a Cluster for consumption by your application workloads. You will write code using these API Objects to define the desired state of your applications and systems deployed into a Kubernetes Cluster.

The defined API Objects communicate the desired state of the workload deployed to the Cluster, and the Cluster has the responsibility of ensuring that desired state becomes the running state of the Cluster.

We will now introduce the core API Objects to define workloads in a Kubernetes Cluster. These are the core building blocks of applications deployed in Kubernetes. In the upcoming sections, we will dive deeper into each of these individually.

- **Pods**: These are container-based applications. A Pod is the unit of work in a Cluster. A Pod is an abstraction that encompasses one or more containers and the resources and configuration it needs to execute, including networking, storage, environment variables, configuration files, and secrets.

- **Controllers**: These define and keep application workloads in the Cluster in the desired state. Some Controllers have the responsibility of starting Pods and keeping those Pods in the desired state. There are several different types of Controllers for ensuring the state of applications and systems deployed and also for the running state of the Cluster. We introduce several Controllers in this section and more throughout the book's remainder, including the Deployment and StatefulSet API Objects.

- **Services**: These provide a networking abstraction for access to Pod-based applications. Services are how applications consumers, such as users and other applications, access the container-based application services deployed in a Cluster via a network.

- **Storage**: This provides an abstraction for Pods to access storage available in a Cluster. Storage is used by applications to persist data independent of the life cycle of Pods.

- **Custom Resource Definition (CRD)**: A CRD is an extension of the Kubernetes API, enabling developers to encapsulate application-specific configuration and functionality in custom API Objects. Then that custom API Object is used to deploy that application. Using CRD allows application developers additional control in how the API Object is defined and functions when deployed. In Azure Arc-enabled Data Services, you will find CRD for SQL Server Managed Instance, PostgreSQL versions 11 and 12, and also for the Data Controller.

In addition to the API Objects described earlier, there are many more used to craft workloads, but these are the core API Object types focused on in this book and for deploying SQL Server and Azure Arc-enabled Data Services.

API Server

The API Server is the central communication hub in a Kubernetes Cluster. It is the primary way users of Kubernetes interact with a Cluster to deploy workloads. It is also the primary way Kubernetes exchanges information between the components inside a Cluster. The API Server is a REST API available over HTTPS exposing API Objects as JSON. As Cluster users define workloads and communicate the information into the API Server, this information is serialized and persisted into the Cluster data store. Kubernetes then will move the running state of the Cluster into the desired state defined in those API Objects stored in the Cluster store. The Cluster data store in Kubernetes is *etcd* which is a distributed key-value data store; for more information, see *https://etcd.io/*.

Core Kubernetes API Primitives

Now it is time to look more closely at each of the high-level API Objects introduced in the last section. This section introduces Pods, Controllers, Services, and Storage. You will learn more details about each and how they enable you to deploy applications in Kubernetes and the workloads that each API Object allows you to deploy.

Pods

A Pod is the most *basic unit of work* in a Kubernetes Cluster. At its core, a Pod is an API Object that represents one or more *containers*, its *resources* such as networking, storage, and *configuration* controlling a Pod's execution. Most commonly, a Pod API Object definition consists of the container image(s), networking ports used to talk to the container-based application, and, if needed, storage.

A Pod is the *unit of scheduling* in a Kubernetes Cluster. In Kubernetes, scheduling determines on which Node in a Cluster to start a Pod. Once the Pod is scheduled on the Node, a container using the specified container image is started on that Node by the container runtime, which conventionally is the containerd container runtime. When scheduling Pods to Nodes, Kubernetes ensures the resources like CPU and memory required to run the Pod are available on the selected Node and, if configured in the Pod, access to the storage.

Note   Kubernetes implements the Container Runtime Interface (CRI), meaning the container runtime is a pluggable resource and can use other CRI compliant container runtimes.

A Pod is the *unit of scaling*. When deploying applications in Kubernetes, you can scale an application horizontally by creating multiple copies of a Pod in a Cluster, called *replicas*. Scaling Pod replicas enables applications to support larger workloads by starting more Pods on the Nodes in a Cluster and leveraging additional Cluster capacity. Further, running multiple replicas of a Pod in a Cluster across multiple Nodes provides high availability in the event of Pod or Node failures.

A Pod is *ephemeral*. If a Pod is deleted, its container(s) on the Node are stopped and then deleted. It is destroyed forever, including its writeable layer. A Pod is never redeployed. Instead, Kubernetes creates a new Pod from the current Pod API Object definition. There is no state maintained between these two deployments of a Pod.

For stateless workloads, like web applications, this is OK. As new Pods are created, when ready, they can begin accepting workload when ready. But for stateful workloads like relational database systems, a Pod needs the ability to persist the state of the data stored in its databases independent of the Pod life cycle. Kubernetes gives us API Objects and constructs for persistent storage which are described later in this chapter.

Controllers

Controllers define, monitor, and keep workloads and the running state of the Cluster in the desired state. This section focuses on Controllers for creating and managing Pods. In Kubernetes, it is rare to create Pods by defining and deploying a Pod Object manually. Two common Workload API Objects are used for deploying applications in Kubernetes. They are *Deployment* and *StatefulSet*.

A Deployment is an API Object that enables you to define an application's desired state in the Pod's configuration and includes the number of Pods to create, called replicas. The Deployment Controller creates a *ReplicaSet*. The ReplicaSet is responsible for starting Pods in the Cluster, using the Pod specification from the Deployment Object. The first frame of Figure 1-1 shows a Deployment that creates a ReplicaSet and that ReplicaSet starts three Pods in the Cluster.

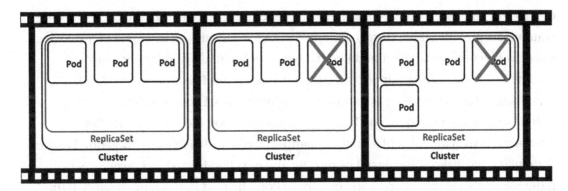

Figure 1-1. *ReplicaSet Operations*

Controllers are responsible for keeping the running state of the Cluster in the desired state, so let's see that in action. In the second frame of Figure 1-1, let's say one of those Pods fails for any reason. Perhaps the application crashed, or maybe even the Node that Pod is running on is no longer available. In the third frame, the ReplicaSet Controller senses that the running state has deviated from desired state and initiates the creation of a new Pod, ensuring the ReplicaSet, or the application, stays in the desired state of three Pods running at all times.

You might be asking, why does the Deployment Controller create a ReplicaSet rather than the Deployment creating the Pods directly? The Deployment Controller defines both the number of Pods to create and also the Pod's configuration. When a Deployment configuration is updated, Pods in the old ReplicaSet shut down, and Pods in a new ReplicaSet are created. This enables the rollout of new container images or Pod configuration. A single Deployment Object still exists, and it manages the declarative updating and transitioning between ReplicaSets. If you want to dig deeper into this topic, check out the Pluralsight course "Managing Kubernetes Controllers and Deployments."

Deployment Controllers do not guarantee order or persistent naming of Pods. A Deployment consists of a collection of Pods, each of which is an exact copy of an application. However, the Pods' names are not persistent if a Pod is destroyed, and a new Pod is created in its place. Applications such as database systems often distribute data across multiple compute elements and then have to keep track of the data's location in the system for subsequent retrieval. Using a Deployment Controller can be problematic for stateful applications that require knowing the precise location of data in a collection of named compute resources.

To allow Kubernetes to support these types of stateful applications, the StatefulSet Controller creates Pods, each with unique, persistent, and ordered names. So, applications that need to control the placement of data across multiple Pods can do that as Pod names are ordered and persist independent of that Pod's life cycle. Further, StatefulSets provide stable storage for applications, ensuring the mapping of the correct storage object to the same named Pod if it has to be created again for any reason.

Figure 1-2 shows an example of a running StatefulSet. This example StatefulSet is defined as having three replicas and creates three Pods. Each Pod it creates has a unique ordered name, sql-0, sql-1, and sql-2. The first Pod created in a StatefulSet always starts with an index of 0. In this example, that's sql-0. For each Pod added to the StatefulSet, the index is increased by one. So, the next Pod is sql-1, followed by sql-2. If the StatefulSet is scaled up to add one more Pod, the next Pod is named sql-3. If the StatefulSet is scaled down, then the highest numbered Pod is removed first. In this example, sql-3 is removed. These ordered creation and scaling operations are essential to stateful applications that place data on named compute resources enabling the stateful applications to know the location of data at any point in time.

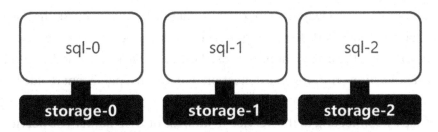

Figure 1-2. *An example StatefulSet – each Pod has a unique, ordered, and persistent name. Each Pod also has persistent storage associated*

In Azure Arc-enabled Data Services, you will find that both SQL Server Managed Instance and PostgreSQL HyperScale use the StatefulSet API Object to provide consistent, ordered naming of Pods and the associated persistent storage.

There are many more Controllers available in Kubernetes. This book focuses on Deployments, ReplicaSets, and StatefulSets and how they are used to deploy Azure Arc-enabled Data Services. There are Controllers to help craft many different types of application workloads in Kubernetes. For more information on different controller types and their functions, check out the Kubernetes documentation at *https://kubernetes. io/docs/concepts/workloads/*.

Services

As we introduced earlier, no Pod is ever recreated. Every time a Pod is created, either during its initial creation or when replacing an existing Pod, that new Pod is assigned a new IP at startup. With Controllers creating and deleting Pods based on configuration, or responding to failures, and affecting the desired state, this leaves us with the challenge of which IP address should be used to access application services provided by Pods running in a Cluster since Pods are assigned an IP address during startup.

Kubernetes provides a networking abstraction for access to Pod-based applications deployed in a Cluster called a *Service*. A Service is a persistent IP address and optionally a DNS name for access into an application running on Pods in a Cluster. Generally speaking, you will have one Service per application deployed in a Cluster. Application traffic received on the Service's IP is load balanced to the underlying Pod IP addresses. As Pods are created and destroyed by Controllers, such as a ReplicaSet Controller, the network information is automatically updated to represent the application's current state. Let's look at an example of this.

In Figure 1-3, let's say a Deployment creates a ReplicaSet, and the ReplicaSet creates three Pods. Each of those Pods has a unique IP address on the network. For users or applications to access the applications in those Pods, a Service is defined. A Service exposes the applications running in a collection of Pods on a persistent IP address and Port, port 80 for HTTP. Users or other applications can access the application provided by that Service by connecting to the Service IP address or DNS name. The Service then load balances that traffic among the Pods that are part of the Service.

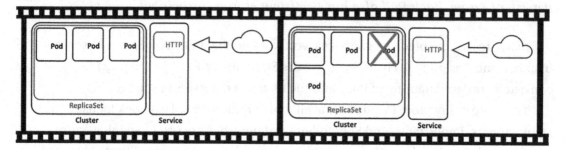

Figure 1-3. *ReplicaSet and Services*

In the second frame of Figure 1-3, let's say one of the Pods in the ReplicaSet fails. The ReplicaSet Controller senses this and deploys a new Pod and registers that new Pod's IP address in the Service and starts load balancing to the new Pod. The Pod that fails is deleted, and its IP address is removed from the Service, and traffic is no longer sent to that IP. This all happens automatically without any user interaction.

Further, when scaling an application up and adding more Pods or scaling an application down by removing some Pods, the Pod IPs are added or removed from the Service accordingly. It truly is a fantastic piece of technology, and we get very excited when we see this in action.

There are three types of Services available in Kubernetes, all of which can be used by Azure Arc-enabled Data Services to access applications running in Kubernetes. The service types are *ClusterIP*, *NodePort*, and *LoadBalancer*. Let's look at each in more detail:

- **ClusterIP**: ClusterIP Services are available *only* inside the Cluster. This type of Service is used when an application does not need to be exposed outside the Cluster.

- **NodePort**: A NodePort Service exposes your application on each Node's real IP address in your Cluster on a fixed port. NodePort Services are accessed using the real network IP addresses of Cluster Nodes combined with the service port. Received traffic is routed to the appropriate Pods supporting the Service. NodePort Services are used when Cluster-based applications need to be accessed outside the Cluster or integrated with external load balancers.

- **LoadBalancer**: This service type integrates cloud provider's load balancer service, or a Cluster external load balancer deployed on-premises such as an F5. A Service of type LoadBalancer is used in cloud-based scenarios when Cluster-based applications need to be accessed outside the Cluster.

Storage

As data professionals, our number one job is keeping data around. And Kubernetes has API Objects to enable the Deployment of stateful applications, like relational database systems. There are two primary API Objects available to help with this, *Persistent Volumes* and *Persistent Volume Claims*.

A Persistent Volume is a storage device available in a Cluster defined by a Cluster administrator available for Pods' consumption. There are many different types of storage available as Persistent Volumes such as virtual disks from cloud providers, iSCSI, NFS, and many more. The implementation details are in the Persistent Volume object. The specific implementation details depend upon the type of storage you want to access. For example, if you want to configure access to an NFS share, you will specify the IP address and export name of the NFS share in the Persistent Volume object.

Pods do not access the Persistent Volume object directly. A Pod uses a Persistent Volume Claim in the Pod Object definition to request Persistent Volume access and capacity. The Persistent Volume Claim will request storage from the Cluster, and then the Persistent Volume Claim will make a claim on the Persistent Volume and mount the Persistent Volume into the Pod file system. This extra layer of abstraction decouples the Pod from the storage implementation details of the Persistent Volume. This has the primary benefit of not having storage implementation details, such as infrastructure-specific storage parameters, as part of the Pod's definition.

Storage Provisioning

There are two different techniques for provisioning storage in a Cluster, *static provisioning* and *dynamic provisioning*.

In static provisioning, a Cluster administrator will define a collection of Persistent Volume Objects in the Cluster. Each object will be a unique storage object that defines the storage device's physical implementation details, such as the location of the storage device on the network and the exact storage volume needed. The Persistent Volume can then be mapped to a Persistent Volume Claim and then allocated to a Pod for use. The key concept here is the Cluster administrator defines each Persistent Volume object and its implementation. This can be cumbersome in large-scale deployments. There's a better way.

Before we get into dynamic provisioning, let us introduce the concept of a Storage Class first. A Storage Class gives Cluster administrators the ability to define storage groups based on the attributes of that storage. Some common groupings include the storage subsystem's performance profile, for example, high-speed storage vs. slower, perhaps less-expensive storage or even from several different types of storage subsystems. Cluster administrators can group types of storage into Storage Classes, and then Persistent Volumes for Pods are dynamically provisioned from a Storage Class.

In dynamic provisioning, there is software installed in your Cluster called a storage provisioner. The provisioner works with your storage infrastructure to dynamically create the Persistent Volume Objects in response to a Persistent Volume Claim created in the Cluster. In the Persistent Volume Claim, you specify the Storage Class you would like to have a Persistent Volume dynamically provisioned from and any configuration parameters required by the storage provisioner.

The key idea in dynamic provisioning is that a Persistent Volume is created dynamically, on demand, in response to the creation of a Persistent Volume Claim rather than being pre-created by an administrator as it is in static provisioning.

From a design standpoint, you can create several Storage Classes in your Cluster, each of which can allocate Persistent Volumes from different types and tiers of storage that is available to your Cluster. You will see later in the book that Azure Arc-enabled Data Services allow you to provision storage from Storage Classes based on the type of data. You will see options to specify a different Storage Class for databases, transaction logs, backups, and also application logs.

Kubernetes Cluster Components

The first part of this chapter introduced Kubernetes concepts and the core API Objects used to build and deploy workloads in a Kubernetes Cluster. Now it is time to dive into what a Kubernetes Cluster is, looking closely at each of the major components.

Exploring Kubernetes Cluster Architecture

A Kubernetes Cluster is a collection of servers (physical or virtual) called *Nodes* that provide a platform for running container-based applications in Pods. There are two types of Nodes in a Cluster. *Control Plane Nodes* are the controller of the Cluster itself, the brains behind the operations. *Worker Nodes* are the compute devices used to run Pods. Let's look at each more closely, starting with the Control Plane Nodes. Figure 1-4 provides us an overview of the Cluster components.

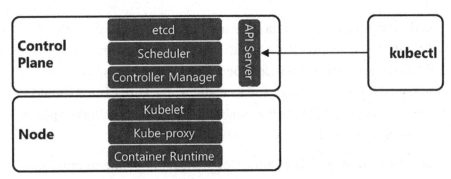

Figure 1-4. *Kubernetes Cluster components*

Control Plane Nodes

Control Plane Nodes operate the Control Plane Services. The Control Plane Services implement the core functions of a Kubernetes Cluster, such as managing the Cluster itself, its resources, and controlling workload. The Control Plane consists of four components, each with a specific responsibility in the Cluster. They are the *API Server*, *etcd*, the *Scheduler*, and the *Controller Manager*. The Control Plane Services and its components are most commonly deployed as Pods that can run on a single Control Plane Node or run on several Control Plane Nodes for high availability. For more information on building highly available Clusters and their configuration, check out *https://kubernetes.io/docs/setup/production-environment/tools/kubeadm/high-availability/* and *https://kubernetes.io/docs/setup/production-environment/tools/kubeadm/ha-topology/*.

Let's look at each of the Control Plane Services and their functions and responsibility in the Cluster in more detail:

- **API Server**: The API Server is the main communication hub in a Cluster. All Cluster components communicate through the API Server to exchange information and state. It is a simple, stateless, REST API that implements and exposes the Kubernetes API for access to users and other Cluster components. As API Objects are created, modified, or deleted, those objects' state is committed to the Cluster. Multiple replicas of the API Server can be deployed across several Control Plane Nodes, and API traffic can be load balanced for high availability.

- **etcd**: etcd is a key-value data store used to persist the state of the Cluster. The API Server itself is stateless but serializes and stores object data in etcd. Since it does persist data, this needs to be protected for both recovery and availability. Backups of etcd should occur frequently, and if high availability is required, multiple replicas are configured in a highly available configuration.

- **Controller Manager**: The Controller Manager implements and ensures the desired state of the Cluster and its workloads. It uses control loops to monitor the running condition continually, compare it with the desired state, and make the changes needed to get the Cluster back into the desired state. To do this, the Controller Manager watches and updates the API Server. Earlier in this chapter, we introduced the Controllers' concept and how they enable you to tell the Kubernetes API what the desired state is. The Controller Manager implements that state. When it comes to Pods and application workloads, if a Deployment defines that three Pod replicas of an application need to be online, the Controller Manager has the responsibility to ensure that those Pods are always online and ready reconciling the defined state with the Cluster's running state by creating new Pods if needed.

- **Scheduler**: The Scheduler decides which Node in a Cluster to start a Pod on. It monitors the API Server looking for any unscheduled Pods. If the Scheduler finds any unscheduled Pods, it determines the best place to run those Pods in the Cluster. The scheduling decision is based on the resources available in the Cluster, the requirements defined for each Pod, and potentially any administrative policy constraints. We will explore the scheduling process in more detail later in this chapter.

Worker Node

Worker Nodes run user application workloads. A Cluster consists of a Control Plane Node and a collection of Worker Nodes. Each Worker Node contributes some amount of CPU and memory resources to the overall available resources in a Cluster. You will need enough CPU and memory resources to run your application workload in a Cluster, ensuring enough capacity for applications and also in the event of Node failures and even growth.

Note   A primary concern for the Control Plane Node is ensuring availability. Check out this link for more information on high-availability Control Plane topologies: *https://kubernetes.io/docs/setup/production-environment/ tools/kubeadm/ha-topology/*.

All Nodes in a Cluster, either Control Plane or Worker, consist of three components, the *kubelet* which communicates with the API Server for Cluster operations, the *kube-proxy* which exposes containers running on that Node to the local network, and the *container runtime* which starts and runs the containers on the Node:

- **kubelet**: The kubelet is a service running on a Node and is responsible for communicating with the API Server, starting Pods on a Node, and ensuring that the Pods on that Node are in a healthy state. The kubelet monitors the API Server for Pod workload state, telling the container runtime to start and stop containers. It also reports back to the API Server the current state of Pods running on a Node and implements health checks on Pods in the form of liveness probes and readiness probes. The kubelet reports back to the API Server the Node's current state and the resources available on that Node.

- **kube-proxy**: kube-proxy is a container running on all Nodes in a Cluster and functions as a network proxy responsible for routing traffic from the network the Node is on to the Pods running on that Node.

- **Container Runtime**: The container runtime is responsible for pulling container images and running containers on the Node. Today, containerd is the most commonly used container runtime used in Kubernetes Clusters. But the Kubernetes container runtime space has moved to using the Container Runtime Interface standard; this enables different container runtimes to be used as the container runtime on Kubernetes Nodes. In this book, the container runtime used is containerd. See *https://kubernetes.io/docs/setup/ production-environment/container-runtimes/* for more information on the container runtimes supported in Kubernetes.

Understanding Scheduling and Resource Allocation

Crucial to successfully deploying workloads in Kubernetes is understanding how Pods are scheduled to Nodes in the Cluster and also how resources are allocated to Pods running on Nodes in a Cluster. In this section, we will dive deeper into each of these topics; let's start off with *scheduling*.

Scheduling in Kubernetes

In Kubernetes, scheduling is the process of selecting a Node in a Cluster to run a Pod. The *Scheduler* is a process that runs on the Control Plane Node in a Kubernetes Cluster. When a Pod is created, the Scheduler assigns the created Pod to start on a specific Node in the Cluster. When finding a Node to run a Pod, the Scheduler considers the resources available, the resource requirements defined on the Pod, and any defined administrative policies. If the Scheduler cannot find an appropriate Node to start a Pod on, the Pod's status is changed to Pending and the Pod is not able to start.

In terms of resources, the Scheduler tries to find the best Node in a Cluster to run a Pod needing to be scheduled. It will look to find a Node in the Cluster that has enough resources to run the Pod. Extending that, if a Node is already running some other number of Pods in its workload, that Node may not have enough resources to run a Pod. Further, if there are no Nodes remaining in the Cluster with any available capacity, then Pods that need to be started will not be able to be scheduled to a Node since no Node with enough available resources is available. In this condition, the status of the Pod changes to Pending and the Pod is not started.

The other element that can influence scheduling is administrative policy. Kubernetes gives Cluster administrators and application developers several tools to influence the scheduling of Pods to Nodes in a Cluster. If the Scheduler cannot find an appropriate Node to start a Pod on based on the defined administrative policies, the Pod's status changes to Pending and the Pod is not started. Let's look closely at several of the tools Cluster administrators and developers can use to influence Pod scheduling; first up is *Requests*:

- **Requests**: Requests are resource guarantees. Using Requests, when defining a workload, you specify an exact amount of CPU or memory a Pod needs to run, and that amount of CPU or memory must be met in order to deploy the Pod on a Node in the Cluster. The Scheduler uses this information to find an appropriate Node to run the Pod. If it is not available, the Pod will not be scheduled and thus not started. We will discuss Requests further in the context of resource management in the next section.

- **Node Selectors**: When defining workloads in Kubernetes, Node Selectors are used to help the Scheduler better understand your physical environment when selecting a Node to run a Pod. For example, if a subset of Nodes in a Cluster has access to specialized hardware resources, perhaps as a high-speed SSD or a GPU, you can use Node Selectors to help the Scheduler understand this configuration, and it can then schedule Pods on only those Nodes. To use Node Selectors, you first assign Labels to those Nodes to identify the fact that they have access to that hardware. Then when defining your Pod, you define a Node Selector looking for Nodes with the assigned Labels. When the Scheduler tries to schedule this workload, it will match the Node Selector to the Node with the desired Label and schedule the newly created Pod to a Node that satisfies the defined Node Selector. In our scenario here, the Pod is scheduled to a Node with the specialized hardware and the application running can then use that hardware. Node Selectors can also be used for physical location targeting which is valuable to ensure Pods can be scheduled across fault domains in a cloud or data center. For more information on Node Selectors, see *https://kubernetes.io/docs/concepts/ scheduling-eviction/assign-pod-node/*.

- **Affinity and Anti-affinity:** Another way to influence which Nodes Pods are scheduled to is Affinity and Anti-affinity. When defining workloads, this technique can give you a greater level of control in how Pods are scheduled. In its most basic implementation, Affinity tells the Scheduler that Pods are to be scheduled on some mutual resource such as a Node or perhaps a fault domain within a cloud or data center. Affinity is often used to ensure the co-location of Pods for applications that require high-performance communications between the Pods. Anti-affinity is the opposite. Anti-affinity ensures that Pods are not co-located on the same resource such as a Node or a fault domain. Anti-affinity is often used to ensure Pods are running on separate resources for either performance or availability reasons. For more information on Affinity and Anti-affinity, see *https:// kubernetes.io/docs/concepts/scheduling-eviction/assign- pod-node/#affinity-and-anti-affinity*.

- **Taints and Tolerations:** This is yet another technique for helping the Scheduler decide which Nodes to schedule Pods. Affinity and Anti-affinity and Node Selectors are used to attract Pods to a Node. Taints and Tolerations are used to repel Pods from Nodes. When a Taint is applied to a Node, no Pods can be scheduled to that Node. A Pod can define a Toleration to a Taint. When a Pod has a Toleration matching a Node's Taint, it can be scheduled to a Node that has a Taint defined. The previously introduced techniques to influence scheduling all require the user deploying the Pod to define constructs in their Deployment to influence the Scheduler. Taints and Tolerations are useful in scenarios where the Cluster administrator needs to influence scheduling without depending on the user deploying the workload. For more information and additional example scenarios, check out *https://kubernetes.io/docs/concepts/scheduling- eviction/taint-and-toleration/*.

For a deeper dive into storage and scheduling in Kubernetes, check out the Pluralsight course "Configuring and Managing Kubernetes Storage and Scheduling" where we cover all of these scenarios in great detail and also with worked examples at *www.pluralsight.com*.

Resource Consumption

By default, Pods will have access to all of the resources available on the Node they are scheduled on. For example, if you have a Node with four cores and 32GB of RAM and SQL Server Pod starts on that Node, the SQL Server process running in that Pod will have access to all four cores and all 32GB of RAM. Due to the nature of how SQL Server allocates and consumes memory, it is possible that a single SQL Server Pod could consume all of the memory available on the Node, especially if Max Server Memory is not set. SQL Server will also be able to schedule workload across all four cores This can lead to resource contention when running multiple Pods on a Node. Kubernetes gives us some configuration parameters to help manage resource consumption in Pods. When defining workloads in Kubernetes, two configuration properties in the Pod spec can help you control resource allocation in Pods deployed in Kubernetes: *Limits* and *Requests*. Let's look at each in more detail:

- **Limits**: For an individual Pod, a Limit is an upper boundary for memory or CPU. Limits are used to ensure that a Pod cannot consume more resources than is appropriate for its workload. When a Limit is set for a Pod, it can only see that amount of memory or CPU. If you create a SQL Server Pod with a memory limit of 16GB of RAM, the SQL Server Pod will see only 16GB of RAM. If you define a CPU limit of two, the SQL Server process will see only two CPUs. Limits are critical for capacity planning. They ensure that you are allocating your Cluster's resources appropriately and not allowing Pods to consume all of the resources on a Node. In our example, if our Nodes have only 32GB of RAM, setting memory and CPU Limits on the Pod will ensure that this Pod will not consume all of the available memory and CPUs on that Node.

- **Requests**: In the previous section, we introduced Requests in the context of scheduling. Let's look more closely at them in the context of resource management. Requests are resource guarantees. With

Requests, we can define the exact amount of CPU or memory a Pod needs to run properly, and that amount of CPU or memory must be available on a Node in the Cluster for that Pod to start. The Scheduler uses this information to find an appropriate Node to run the Pod. If it is not available, the Pod will neither be scheduled nor started. Requests are used to ensure that a Pod has the appropriate amount of resources to run its workload and never any less.

Using Limits and Requests gives you the ability to ensure workloads running share the resources of the Cluster using appropriate resources and also ensure your workloads have access to the resource needed. When defining workloads with Azure Arc-enabled Data Services, both SQL Managed Instance and PostgreSQL Hyperscale deployments give you the ability to set both Limits and Requests on the Pods created. It is recommended that you *always* set both a Limit and a Request when defining workloads to help ensure a well-performing and well-balanced workload in your Cluster.

Tip   For a closer look at how SQL Server and Kubernetes memory management works, check out *www.centinosystems.com/blog/sql/memory-settings-for-running-sql-server-in-kubernetes/*.

Networking Fundamentals

The final major topic in our Kubernetes primer chapter is networking. The Kubernetes networking model enables workloads to be deployed in Kubernetes while abstracting away network complexities. This simplifies application configuration and service discovery in a Cluster and increases the portability of deployment code by removing infrastructure-specific code. This section introduces the Kubernetes networking model and example Cluster communication patterns.

Three rules govern Kubernetes' networking. These rules enable the simplicity described earlier. These rules are from *https://kubernetes.io/docs/concepts/cluster-administration/networking/*.

Kubernetes Network Model Rules

1. All Pods can communicate with each other on all Nodes without Network Address Translation (NAT).

2. All agents, such as system daemons and the kubelet, on a Node, can communicate with all Pods on that Node.

3. Pods in the host network of a Node can communicate with all Pods on all Nodes without NAT.

The preceding rules simplify networking and application configuration by ensuring Pods are talking to each other on the actual Pod IPs and container ports rather than having them translated to an IP scheme dependent upon the network infrastructure where they are deployed.

In Kubernetes, a Pod Network is the network Pods are attached to when the container runtime starts them on a Node. Each Pod deployed is given a unique IP address on the Pod Network. Pod Networks must follow the rules defined earlier, which result in Pods using their real IP addresses. When implementing Pod Networks, there are many solutions to ensure adherence to the Kubernetes networking model rule. A common solution is overlay networking, which uses a tunneling protocol to exchange packets between Nodes independent of the underlying physical infrastructure's network. This enables the overlay network to use a layer 3 IP scheme independent of the data center's physical infrastructure, enabling simpler adherence to the Kubernetes networking model.

Another option is to build a Pod Network as part of a data center infrastructure as part of a bare-metal approach. This will require the coordination of the Kubernetes Cluster administrator and the network engineering team responsible for the network.

The following are common communication patterns used in a Kubernetes Cluster showing Pods accessing each other and also accessing the Services provided by Pods. Chapter 4 introduces Pod Networks during the Cluster installation process, and Chapter 6 will dive into Services and how traffic is routed to Pods in the Pod Network.

Communication Patterns

Figure 1-5 shows some example communication patterns in a Kubernetes Cluster. Let's walk through each of those together:

1. **Inside a Pod.**
   Multiple containers within a Pod share the same container Namespace. These containers can communicate with each other over localhost on unique ports.

2. **Pod to Pod within a Node.**
   When Pods on the same Node need to communicate over the network, they do so over a local software bridge defined on the Node and use the Pod IP.

3. **Pod to Pod on another Node.**
   When Pods on different Nodes need to communicate over the network, they do so over the local layer 2 or layer 3 network using the Pod IP.

4. **Services.**
   When accessing Services in a Cluster, traffic is routed to the kube-proxy implementing that Service and then routed to the Pod providing that application service. As introduced earlier in this chapter, Services will be your most common interaction with applications deployed in a Cluster.

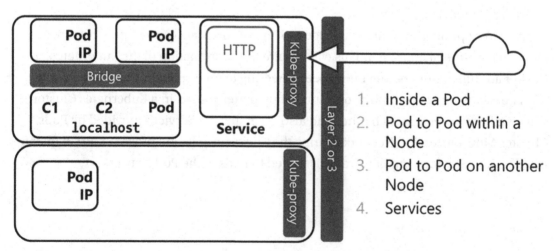

Figure 1-5. Kubernetes networking

Kubernetes Role in Azure Arc-enabled Data Services

Over the last few years, the SQL Server Engineering Team has released some exciting technologies and innovations – SQL Server on Linux, SQL Server on containers, SQL Server on Kubernetes, and Azure Data Studio – and we couldn't help but wonder, why? What's the big picture on all of these seemingly disparate technologies? The first time we saw the SQL Server Product Team demonstrate Azure Arc-enabled Data Services is when we had that a-ha! moment. It's not the cool factor of each of these individual technologies, but what bringing all of these technologies together enables. Running any Data Service, anywhere you have Kubernetes.

Running Data Services inside Kubernetes enables Microsoft to define systems in code. You can then run that code anywhere you have Kubernetes because of the infrastructure abstraction that it provides. The Kubernetes API is essentially a wrapper around the resources in your data center or cloud. The code written to deploy systems can work anywhere that API is implemented on, in any cloud, in edge sites, or even on-premises data centers. Throughout the remainder of this book, we will show you the value proposition of Azure Arc-enabled Data Services and how to deploy and manage those Azure Arc-enabled Data Services anywhere you have Kubernetes.

Summary and Key Takeaways

This chapter introduced Kubernetes and how it enables the deployment of modern container-based applications. You learned how the Kubernetes API allows you to build and model applications deployed into a Kubernetes Cluster. You also learned the core API primitives for deploying workloads; Pods, your container-based application; Controllers, keeping the Cluster and its workload in the desired state; Services, for access to the applications; and storage, for stateful applications. Then you learned the components of a Cluster and how they work together to ensure that your desired state is implemented and a quick tour of scheduling, resource management, and the Kubernetes network model. With all that theory behind us, now it's time to move into the next chapter where we will introduce Azure Arc-enabled Data Services discussing the challenges it solves and dive into its architecture, core features, how workloads are deployed and managed, and also key deployment considerations.

CHAPTER 2

Azure Arc-enabled Data Services

This chapter introduces you to Azure Arc-enabled Data Services! Starting off, you will learn some of the challenges of a modern hybrid cloud, and we will then show you how Azure Arc addresses those challenges to provide manageability at scale in on-premises or in any cloud. Next, we will introduce the core Azure Arc-enabled resources, including Servers, Kubernetes, SQL Server, and Data Services. We will then dive deeper into what Azure Arc-enabled Data Services are, its architecture, how workloads are deployed and managed, and discuss key deployment considerations such as compute and storage capacity planning.

The Challenge

- Hybrid cloud is becoming the new normal in enterprise system architectures. According to the *Flexera 2020 State of the Cloud* (see `www.flexera.com/about-us/press-center/flexera-releases-2020-state-of-the-cloud-report.html`) report, nearly 87% of enterprises have a hybrid cloud strategy. There are several variations of hybrid cloud. First, organizations can adopt a hybrid cloud strategy with assets in more than one public cloud, such as Amazon Web Service (AWS), Google Cloud, and Microsoft Azure. This pattern is oftentimes called "multi-cloud." The second type of hybrid cloud strategy is organizations having some cloud assets

© Ben Weissman and Anthony E. Nocentino 2022
B. Weissman and A. E. Nocentino, *Azure Arc-enabled Data Services Revealed*,
https://doi.org/10.1007/978-1-4842-8085-0_2

and some on-premises. In these scenarios, organizations generally
will put the parts of their infrastructure that can benefit from the
cloud the most in the cloud. Primary reasons for companies to go
to the cloud include elasticity, automation, built-in monitoring and
security, and pay-as-you-go payment models.

When managing and operating a hybrid cloud environment, either multi-cloud or
on-premises and cloud, the management, security models, and tools are likely different
across each of the environments. And this begs the question, how do you manage these
environments at scale? Enabling consistency and control is challenging when you have
different management, monitoring, security, and deployment tools. The goal of Azure
Arc is to enable consistency across all of these areas, homogenizing the management,
monitoring, and security services and also the deployment tooling so that you can
leverage the benefits of cloud wherever you have resources deployed, on-premises or in
any cloud.

Introducing Azure Arc

At its core, Microsoft Azure Arc provides Azure management services wherever you
have deployed resources on-premises or any cloud. It enables you to have consistent
management services and tooling for your organizations' core operations across
technology architectures wherever deployed. Let's look at the core features of Azure Arc:

- **Unified Experience Across On-Premises and Hybrid Cloud**:
  Familiar tools like the Azure Portal, azure-cli, PowerShell, and REST
  API are available to you to manage and deploy systems.

- **Deployment and Operations**: With a unified set of tools,
  deployments and operations are consistent wherever you deploy, on-
  premises or in any cloud. Unified tooling enables your organization
  to use the same code and tools in any deployment scenario wherever
  deployed. A pivotal element to operations is performance and
  availability monitoring, and Azure Monitor is available to help you do
  that for your Azure Arc-enabled resources.

- **Consolidated Access Controls, Security, Policy Management, and Logging**: Implementing more than one security model based on where your resources are deployed is challenging and risky since you potentially have to manage multiple sets of security rules and their implementations. Azure Arc enables you to have a consolidated security model and implementation and use tools like Azure Log Analytics for centralized security and application logs. Additionally, you can manage governance and control solutions with services like Azure Policy.

- **Inventory and Organization**: With one set of tooling available and key Azure constructs such as resource groups, subscription, and tags, administrators, operators, and managers can get a complete view of their technology estate regardless of where systems are deployed as services and resources are registered as managed resources in Azure irrespective of where they are deployed, on-premises or in any cloud.

Now that we've introduced you to the core features of Azure Arc, it is time to move forward and take a closer look at the resources that you can manage and deploy using Azure Arc.

Azure Arc-enabled Resources

The focus of this book is Azure Arc-enabled Data Services. Azure Arc-enabled Data Services are part of a broader strategy that provides a Control Plane over resources wherever deployed, on-premises or in any cloud. Azure Arc achieves this goal by extending Azure Resource Manager (ARM) to these resources. ARM is the Management Control Plane used in the Azure Public Cloud. ARM provides deployment, organization, and access control to resources deployed in the Azure Cloud. Azure Arc extends ARM to wherever you have resources deployed, on-premises or in any cloud. At the time of writing this book, there are four key resources that can be managed by Azure Arc: *Azure Arc-enabled Servers, Azure Arc-enabled Kubernetes, Azure Arc-enabled SQL Servers*, and *Azure Arc-enabled Data Services*. Figure 2-1 introduces the elements of Azure Arc; let's walk through each of these core services in more detail.

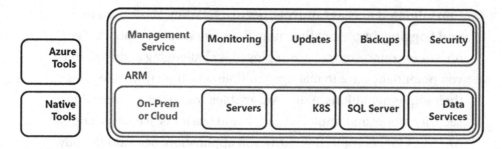

Figure 2-1. Azure Arc Architecture

Azure Arc-enabled Servers

Azure Arc-enabled Servers provides management capabilities for both Windows and Linux operating systems deployed on physical and virtual machines (VMs) hosted outside of Azure. Servers connect to Azure using a locally installed agent and become resources that are managed using standard Azure tools and management services. The core management capabilities for Azure Arc-enabled Servers include inventory, policy, deployment automation, configuration management, performance monitoring, security and access controls, centralized logging, and update management. For more information on Azure Arc-enabled Servers, visit *https://docs.microsoft.com/en-us/azure/azure-arc/servers/overview*.

Azure Arc-enabled Kubernetes

Kubernetes is the standard for deploying enterprise grade container-based applications. Azure Arc-enabled Kubernetes enables management of Cloud Native Computing Foundation (CNCF) certified Kubernetes Clusters wherever they are deployed including upstream Kubernetes, RedHat OpenShift, AWS EKS, Google GKE, among others. The key management features of Azure Arc-enabled Kubernetes are inventory management, policy management, centralized logging, performance monitoring, application deployment, and Cluster configuration.

A key scenario enabled by Azure Arc-enabled Kubernetes is GitOps-based configuration management. GitOps enables application deployment and Cluster configuration by using GitOps-based configuration management. Configuration artifacts are checked into a Git repository, and the Arc Cluster agent monitors that Git repository for configuration changes. As configurations are checked into the repo, the

Cluster agent will deploy that change locally in the Kubernetes Cluster. This enables strong configuration management since all configuration artifacts, for both Cluster configuration and application deployment, are checked into the repository and source controlled. Test, review, and approval workflows can be built around the source control system. If the Cluster skews away from what is checked into the repository, the checked in configuration will be asserted on the Cluster to bring it back into the desired state.

Check out *https://docs.microsoft.com/en-us/azure/azure-arc/kubernetes/ overview* for more information and supported Kubernetes distributions.

Azure Arc-enabled SQL Server

The next Azure Arc-enabled service we want to introduce is Azure Arc-enabled SQL Server. Azure Arc-enabled SQL Server enables you to extend Azure management services to SQL Server instances wherever deployed, on-premises or in any cloud. An agent is installed on the SQL Server instance, and the SQL Server is then registered with Azure. The SQL Server instance is then managed using standard Azure tools and management services. The core management features are inventory management, policy management, centralized logging, security, and threat protection via services like Azure Security Center and Azure Sentinel.

Further, in Azure Arc-enabled SQL Server, environment checks are implemented using SQL Assessments. SQL Assessments are a collection of industry-standard best practices that can be used to assess and report the overall environment health of a SQL Server instance or a group of SQL Server instances. Azure Arc-enabled SQL Server combined with Azure Arc-enabled Servers can give you a rich management experience for both SQL Server and the underlying operating system. For more information on Azure Arc-enabled SQL Server, check out *https://docs.microsoft.com/en-us/sql/ sql-server/azure-arc/overview*.

We want to take a moment to call out the Azure Arc-enabled SQL Server and Azure Arc-enabled Data Services are unique offerings under the Azure Arc umbrella. Azure Arc-enabled SQL Server extends Azure management services to traditional deployments of installed instances of SQL Server. Azure Arc-enabled Data Services give you the ability to deploy Azure Platform as a Service (PaaS)-based services on-premises or in any cloud.

Azure Arc-enabled Data Services

Last but not least and the likely reason you're reading this book is Azure Arc-enabled Data Services. Azure Arc-enabled Data Services provide you the ability to deploy traditionally Azure Platform as a Service (PaaS)-based services on-premises or in any cloud. The value that data services provide is an always current deployment model delivering to you the most up-to-date, secure, and supported versions of Azure PaaS Data Services wherever you need to deploy. The data services available at the time of this book writing include *Azure Arc-enabled SQL Managed Instance* and *Azure Arc-enabled PostgreSQL Hyperscale*. Additional capabilities of Azure Arc-enabled Data Services include elastic scale, self-service provisioning, inventory management, deployment automation, update management, managed backups, security, performance monitoring, and centralized logging. Azure Arc-enabled Data Services are the core focus of this book, and we will dig into the core functions throughout the remainder of this book.

Tooling

So far, we have focused on how Azure Arc can manage resources wherever they are. Now it's time to focus on the tools that you can use to manage resources. First, we will introduce Azure tools, such as the Azure Portal, azure-cli, PowerShell, and Azure Data Studio. However, Microsoft's approach ensures that you have a choice in the tools you can use to manage your cloud and developer experience. So, industry-standard, open source tools that you maybe are already using in your projects. We will then introduce how application native tools can be used to manage applications and services deployed in Azure Arc.

Azure Tools

One of the key challenges Azure Arc attempts to solve is consistent tooling. Azure Arc extends Azure Resource Manager to wherever your resources are deployed, on-premises or in any cloud. Since ARM is available, this enables you to use the standard Azure tools you are used to using in the Azure Public Cloud. Let's walk through a listing of the most common Azure tools you will use in Azure Arc and Azure Arc-enabled Data Services:

- **Azure Portal**: Key to the Azure management experience is the Azure Portal. Resources that are registered and managed by Azure and Azure Arc will appear in the Azure Portal. The Azure Portal will be a primary way to manage your Arc-enabled resources. You can view information collected and exposed in the Azure Portal in the various Azure management services such as Log Analytics, Monitor, Sentinel, Security Center, and more. For more information, visit *https:// portal.azure.com.*

- **azure-cli**: azure-cli is the command-line interface to deploy and manage Azure Resource Manager (ARM)-enabled resources including Azure Arc-enabled Data Service. For more information, visit *https://docs.microsoft.com/en-us/cli/azure/install-azure-cli.*

- **Azure PowerShell**: The Azure PowerShell Module (Az Module) is a PowerShell module used to manage Azure Resource Manager (ARM)-enabled resources. For more information, visit *https:// docs.microsoft.com/en-us/powershell/azure/new-azureps-module-az.*

- **Azure Data Studio (ADS)**: This is the cross-platform tool providing modernized experiences across an array of Azure Data Services. In ADS, you will find deployment and management experiences for both Azure Arc-enabled Data Services and SQL Server Big Data Clusters. Additionally, you will find a SQL Server code editor with built-in source control integration using Git. For more information, visit *https://docs.microsoft.com/en-us/sql/azure-data-studio/.*

Native Tools

A primary goal of Azure Arc is to homogenize the management and tools enabling your organization to have a better cloud experience. Important to note is that you can still use your current developer experiences as well as the tools you are using today to manage your cloud. So, if you have existing deployment pipelines in place, this is OK; you can still use those in Azure Arc-enabled Data Services. Leaving the choice in how you want to manage your workloads up to you. We want to take a second to call out tools you may already use to manage your environments. These tools, among others, form the foundation of modern deployment pipelines:

- **kubectl/oc:** These are the primary command-line tools for controlling Kubernetes and RedHat OpenShift Clusters.

- **helm:** This is a tool for defining how to deploy complex applications in Kubernetes using pre-configured templates called helm charts.

- **Git/GitHub:** Git has become a standard way to manage source code. Key to the design of Azure Arc is enabling you to use your existing tools for your deployment pipelines which means you are still able to use your existing code management and deployment experiences.

- **GitOps:** As introduced earlier, GitOps enables you to store your Cluster and application deployment state as configuration artifacts in a Git repository. Kubernetes Clusters monitor the repository for changes and affect those changes in the Cluster to maintain the system's desired state.

The data services available in Azure Arc-enabled Data Services are SQL Managed Instance and PostgreSQL Hyperscale. When deploying with Azure Native Tools, you will use the appropriate portal experiences or command-line syntax to create and manage data services deployments. These experiences are covered in great detail throughout the remainder of the book.

For deploying and managing data services workloads with Kubernetes native tools, the SQL Server Engineering Team has taken a cloud-native approach and created Custom Resource Definitions for each of the Azure Arc-enabled Data Services, the Data Controller itself, and management tasks such as database restore operations. A Custom Resource Definition is a Kubernetes construct that allows developers to extend the Kubernetes API and create custom API Objects. Custom Resource Definitions can have additional configuration, data, or even controlling the behavior of the object in the Cluster. So, when defining workloads using Kubernetes native tooling, these Custom Resource Definition API Objects are used. Now that we have covered the tools used for deployment, let's move on and look more closely at the Azure Arc-enabled Data Services that can be deployed.

Introducing Azure Arc-enabled Data Services

In this section, we will begin by introducing the Azure Arc-enabled Data Services Architecture. Then next, we'll introduce the PaaS-based Data Services available, specifically SQL Managed Instance and PostgreSQL Hyperscale. Then to close out this section, we will introduce the deployment techniques and deployment considerations when designing a solution focusing on compute and storage resources.

Azure Arc-enabled Data Services Architecture

Azure Arc-enabled Data Services Architecture is a layered architecture of hardware, Kubernetes, Management/Control Plane, and Data Services. Figure 2-2 highlights the architecture.

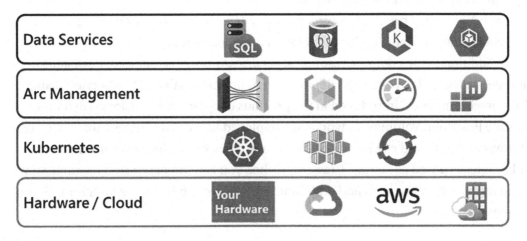

Figure 2-2. *Azure Arc-enabled Data Services Architecture is a layered architecture of hardware, Kubernetes, Management, and deployed Data Services*

The foundational layer is hardware which can be either on-premises or in any cloud and built on either physical or virtual machines. Then next, Kubernetes is deployed on that hardware. And as we learned in the previous chapter, Kubernetes enables you to quickly and consistently deploy applications in code in the Cluster. Then, deployed inside the Kubernetes Cluster is the Arc Management Control Plane. The Arc Management Control Plane is Azure Arc's brains and extends Azure Resource Manager (ARM) to your on-premises or hybrid cloud deployments. And on top of all of that is

Azure Arc-enabled Data Services. These are the traditionally PaaS-based offerings that you can deploy anywhere you have Azure Arc, on-premises or in any cloud. Now, let's look at each layer of this architecture in more detail.

Hardware Layer

The Azure Arc Data Services Architecture is built on *physical or virtual machine-based servers*. Each server contributes some amount of CPU and memory capacity for applications to run on. As introduced in the previous chapter on Kubernetes, a Kubernetes Cluster server is called a Node. Each Node's number and size depend on the size requirements of the workload deployed and some additional capacity for a Node's failure in the Kubernetes Cluster. Further, you can expand and contract the amount of resources in a Kubernetes Cluster by adding or removing servers. We will explore this topic in more detail later in this chapter.

Each Node must run the *Linux operating system* since all of the containers running in Azure Arc-enabled Data Services are Linux-based containers.

In addition to the compute resources, *persistent storage* is required. Persistent storage is allocated to workloads deployed in Azure Arc-enabled Data Services using the storage constructs introduced in the previous chapter. Storage Classes dynamically allocate Persistent Volumes for workloads deployed in the Kubernetes Cluster. The type of storage provisioned can be any of the storage types supported by your version of Kubernetes exposed as Storage Classes. Further, you can increase the allocatable storage capacity in a Cluster or even add additional storage types by defining additional Storage Classes.

Kubernetes Layer

With the underlying hardware in place, the next layer in the architecture is Kubernetes. Kubernetes, regardless of distribution, provides a consistent API for building workloads, and because of this, Azure Arc-enabled Data Services support several Kubernetes distributions. Supported distributions include open source/upstream Kubernetes Clusters built with kubeadm and commercial distributions like RedHat's OpenShift.

At the time of writing, there are several *supported Kubernetes distributions* based on the deployment mechanism:

- Open source, upstream Kubernetes, deployed with kubeadm

- OpenShift Container Platform (OCP)

Several *managed service offerings* are supported:

- Azure Kubernetes Service (AKS)

- Azure Kubernetes Service (AKS) on Azure Stack

- Azure Kubernetes Service (AKS) on Azure Stack HCI

- Azure RedHat OpenShift (ARO)

- AWS Elastic Kubernetes Service (EKS)

- Google Cloud Kubernetes Engine (GKE)

Note   For more information on specific versions of the various Kubernetes distributions supported, please check out this link: `https://docs.microsoft.com/en-us/azure/azure-arc/kubernetes/validation-program`.

The key concept here is that you can deploy Azure Arc-enabled Data Services on any distribution of Kubernetes anywhere you need to deploy, on-premises or in a hybrid cloud scenario. You have the choice of using upstream/open source Kubernetes and also many of the managed service offerings. Once you have Kubernetes up and running, the next thing to do is extend Azure into your Cluster by deploying an Azure Arc Data Services Data Controller.

Azure Arc Management Control Plane Layer

With Kubernetes deployed, the next layer in the architecture is the Arc Management Control Plane Layer which extends Azure's management capabilities to your on-premises or hybrid cloud environment. At this layer, in Azure Arc-enabled Data Services, a *Data Controller* is deployed. The Data Controller is deployed as a Custom Resource in Kubernetes. The Data Controller implements core functionality such as Azure Arc Integration and management services. Let's look closer at each of these.

The Azure Arc Integration is what sends logging, performance, and usage information back into Azure based on the data services workloads deployed. The Data Controller extends Azure Resource Manager to your on-premises or hybrid cloud deployment and lights up the Azure Arc-enabled services to manage the deployed applications and resources. The management services implemented by the Data Controller include a Controller Service and API Endpoint, provisioning management,

management and performance dashboards, metrics, logging, managed backup/restore, and high-availability service coordination. We will dive deeper into the Data Controller and its core functions in an upcoming section. With the Controller online, the next layer in the architecture is to deploy data services workloads.

Note   We want to call out that the Data Controller is for managing Azure Arc-enabled Data Services. Azure Arc-enabled Servers, Kubernetes, and SQL Servers each rely on agents installed on the Azure Arc-managed resources.

Data Services Layer

The final layer in an Azure Arc-enabled Data Services Architecture is the data services themselves. Azure Arc-enabled Data Services enable you to self-provision traditionally Azure Public Cloud PaaS-based services like SQL Managed Instance and PostgreSQL Hyperscale in our on-premises or hybrid cloud environments on Kubernetes. *Azure Arc-enabled SQL Managed Instance* is your lift-and-shift version of SQL Server, enabling you to move workloads seamlessly into Azure Arc-enabled Data Services as it provides a high level of compatibility with on-premises installations of SQL Server. Next, *Azure Arc-enabled PostgreSQL Hyperscale* is the leading open source database used as a data store for mission-critical applications. PostgreSQL Hyperscale is an implementation in Azure that enables you to horizontally scale data by sharding it across multiple instances and allows for distributed parallel query execution. These data services are deployed as resources in Kubernetes and are managed by the Data Controller.

To recap, essentially, wherever you have hardware and deploy Kubernetes and a Data Controller, Azure Arc-enabled Data Services can be deployed.

Azure Arc Management Control Plane Layer: A Closer Look

Now it is time to take a closer look at the Azure Arc Management Control Plane. To extend Azure Services from the cloud to on-premises or hybrid cloud environments, a Data Controller is deployed in your Kubernetes Cluster. The Data Controller implements Azure Arc integrations and several key on-premises management functions. This section will introduce the Data Controller's connectivity modes, its core functions, and how its operations and management capabilities differ based on the connectivity mode in use.

A Data Controller's *connectivity mode* defines how a Data Controller exchanges data with the Azure Public Cloud and also defines which management services are deployed within the Kubernetes Cluster and which Azure Services are used to manage data services in the Cluster. There are two connectivity modes for the Data Controller, *indirectly connected* and *directly connected* mode. Which connectivity mode you should choose is based on your deployment's technical and security requirements and possibly business rules or government regulations. Let's look more closely at each connectivity mode.

Indirectly Connected Mode

In indirectly connected mode, there is no direct connection from the Data Controller in your Cluster to the Azure Public Cloud. The local Data Controller itself functions as the primary point of management and deployment for data services in your Kubernetes Cluster. For deploying and managing workloads, all operations are governed by the local Data Controller in your Cluster. Additionally, all management functions are implemented inside the local Cluster. For example, performance metrics and logging web portals and data stores are implemented as Pods running in your local Kubernetes Cluster. Further, critical data services managed operations such as update management, automated backup/restore, and high-availability coordination are implemented at this layer. Figure 2-3 highlights the architecture of indirectly connected mode where the Data Controller does not have a persistent connection into the Azure Cloud.

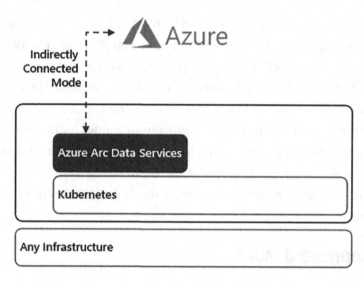

Figure 2-3. *Indirectly connected mode – there is no direct connection from the Data Controller into the Azure Cloud. Data is exchanged via an import/export process using azure-cli*

In indirectly connected mode, inventory, performance, logging, and usage data can be exported to files and then uploaded to Azure. Once uploaded into Azure, the deployed Azure Arc-enabled Data Services will be visible as resources in the Azure Portal. Further, Azure Services, such as Metrics, Log Analytics, and more, can be used to analyze the data exported from the on-premises or hybrid cloud environment. It is possible to schedule this export/upload process at a periodic interval so that the data is uploaded and available inside Azure, giving the appearance of continuous uploading of data. Azure Services that require direct connectivity are not available.

In indirectly connected mode, data services deployment and configuration changes are sent to the Kubernetes API running on the Data Controller using tools such as Azure Data Studio; azure-cli (az); Kubernetes native tools like kubectl, helm, or oc; and also Azure Arc-enabled Kubernetes GitOps. If Kubernetes native tools are used, these deployments are sent directly to the Kubernetes API. In indirectly connected mode, deployments and configuration changes cannot be made using the Azure Portal, ARM APIs, and ARM templates. However, Azure Services such as inventory management, metrics, and logging are available due to the export process described earlier.

Typical scenarios for this connectivity mode are that data centers with business or security policies do not allow for outbound connectivity or data uploads to external services. Other deployments that can use indirectly connected mode include edge site locations with intermittent Internet connectivity.

Directly Connected Mode

In directly connected mode, Azure itself becomes the Control Plane for coordinating management and deployment functions in your Azure Arc-enabled Data Services environment. In this connectivity mode, the Kubernetes Cluster you are deploying Azure Arc-enabled Data Services into needs to be an Azure Arc-enabled Kubernetes Cluster. By connecting your Kubernetes Cluster to Azure, Azure Arc agents are deployed into your Cluster. These agents have the responsibility of persisting an outbound connection to Azure and exchanging information with Azure such as metrics, logs, and usage data as well as enabling a richer Azure management experience with additional Azure Services when compared with indirectly connected mode. When using directly connected mode, a persistent network connection is initiated from the customer environment out to the Azure Cloud over secure, encrypted channels. If there is an interruption in connectivity, the operations are queued locally and pushed into Azure when connectivity is restored.

In directly connected mode, deployment and configuration changes can be created using the Azure Portal, ARM APIs, azure-cli, Azure PowerShell, and ARM templates as addition to the tools used in indirectly connected mode. Figure 2-4 highlights the architecture of directly connected mode where the Azure Arc-enabled Kubernetes agent has a direct, sustained connection into the Azure Cloud and is constantly uploading metrics, logs, and usage data as well as enabling a richer Azure management experience with additional Azure Services. Common scenarios for this connectivity mode are for managing deployments in other public clouds, edge site locations, and corporate data centers that have policies that allow such connectivity.

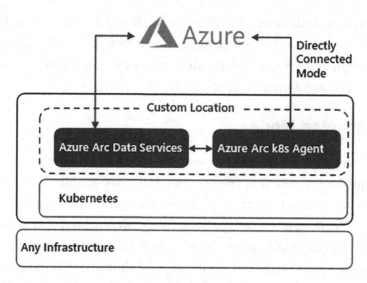

Figure 2-4. *Directly connected mode – the Azure Arc-enabled Kubernetes agent maintains a persistent, secure connection into the Azure Cloud for exchanging configuration state and monitoring and logging data*

When using directly connected mode, in addition to Azure Arc-enabling your Kubernetes Cluster, you will need the Azure Arc-enabled Data Services Cluster Extension deployed into your Cluster. A Cluster Extension controls the Azure capabilities of your Kubernetes Cluster such as the Azure Services it offers as well as the version and life cycle of those services. The Azure Arc-enabled Data Services Cluster Extension is used to create the Custom Resource Definitions for the Azure Arc-enabled Data Services and their capabilities and bootstrapping Cluster deployment.

When working with Azure Resources, traditionally you deploy resources in a region. To extend that concept into a hybrid scenario, reaching compute resources outside of Azure, you need to define a custom location. A custom location is a pointer from Azure to a Kubernetes Namespace defined in an Azure Arc-enabled Kubernetes Cluster (see Figure 2-5).

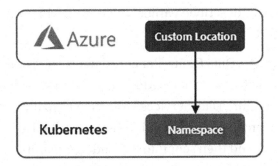

Figure 2-5. *Concept of custom locations*

This custom location is used by administrators as target locations for the deployment of Azure Arc-enabled Data Services on your local compute resources. The process of Azure Arc enabling your Kubernetes Cluster is covered in detail in Chapter 6 as part of the process of creating a directly connected Azure Arc-enabled Data Services Data Controller.

Note   For more details on the management services and the network connectivity, such as Internet addresses, ports, and proxy server support, check out *https://docs.microsoft.com/en-us/azure/azure-arc/data/ connectivity*.

Azure Arc-enabled Data Services Management Functions

Inside the Arc Management Control Plane, a Data Controller and locally available management functions are deployed. In this section, we will walk you through each of those core elements. Figure 2-6 highlights these management functions as deployed inside a local Kubernetes Cluster.

- **Controller Service**: This is the management endpoint available in your Kubernetes Cluster responsible for handling management operations.

- **API**: The Data Controller exposes an API that can interact with your Kubernetes Cluster for management operations such as exporting performance, logging, or usage data to upload to Azure. Deployment operations are done via the Kubernetes API directly or using the deployment tools described earlier which in turn interact with the Kubernetes API.

- **Provisioning**: The Data Controller coordinates provisioning operations with the Kubernetes API. When working with Kubernetes native tools or Azure Data Services tools such as Azure Data Studio and azure-cli, provisioning operations are submitted directly to the Kubernetes API and then sent into the underlying Kubernetes Cluster to deploy new workloads and configuration state changes. The Data Controller monitors provisioning requests for Custom Resources, such as SQL Managed Instance and Postgres, and coordinates with the Kubernetes API to provision the supporting Kubernetes native objects such as StatefulSets, Services, and others that make up the Custom Resource being deployed.

- **Dashboards**: Management dashboards are available in Azure Data Studio. These dashboards provide information on the current state of the data services deployed and the Data Controller itself.

- **Metrics**: Grafana is used to expose key performance metrics at several layers in your Cluster, including PostgreSQL Hyperscale and SQL Server Managed Instance-specific dashboards. Grafana is available as a web portal deployed in your Cluster.

- **Logging**: Kibana is used to aggregate and provide search capabilities for logs emitted in the Cluster. Several resources are streaming log data into Kibana including SQL Managed and PostgreSQL Hyperscale instances deployed. Kibana is available as a web portal deployed in your Cluster.

- **Managed Backup and Restore**: Backup and restore automation are controlled by the Data Controller. Every Azure Arc-enabled SQL Managed Instance comes with a built-in automatic backup feature which is enabled by default. This means that every single database that gets created or restored will automatically receive an initial full backup followed by scheduled differential and transaction log backups. This concept is very similar to the managed backup in an Azure SQL Managed Instance and allows you to perform a point-in-time restore to any specific timestamp within your retention period.

- **High Availability**: Kubernetes provides basic high availability for workloads managed by Controllers such as ReplicaSets and StatefulSets. If a Pod controlled by one of these controllers fails, the new Pod will be created in the Cluster replacing the failed Pod. For more advanced scenarios that might require coordinated failover events for Pods inside the Cluster, the Data Controller can facilitate this application-aware failover event.

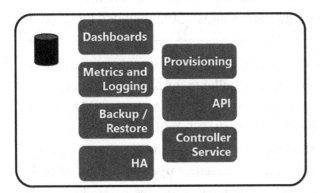

Figure 2-6. *Azure Arc Management Control Plane implements many of core management and operations functions in your local Kubernetes Cluster*

Data Services Layer: A Closer Look

With all of the required infrastructure in place, hardware, Kubernetes, and a Data Controller, it is now time to focus on the data services layer. This layer is where you deploy traditionally PaaS-based Data Services, such as those that you see in the Azure Cloud, in your environment wherever it is on-premises or in any cloud. This section digs deeper into each of the currently available data services, Azure Arc-enabled SQL Managed Instance and Azure Arc-enabled PostgreSQL Hyperscale, looking at their capabilities and value.

Azure Arc-enabled SQL Managed Instance

Azure Arc-enabled SQL Managed Instance is your lift-and-shift version of SQL Server. It enables you to move workloads seamlessly into Azure Arc as it provides a high level of compatibility with on-premises installations of SQL Server, which is documented as nearly 100% compatible. This means that to move your databases from their current on-premises implementations into Azure Arc-enabled SQL Managed Instance will require little to no database changes. When deploying an Azure Arc-enabled SQL Managed Instance, you can take a backup from an on-premises version of SQL Server and restore that backup directly to an Azure Arc-enabled SQL Managed Instance.

Tip   Following *https://docs.microsoft.com/en-us/azure/azure-arc/ data/managed-instance-features#Unsupported*, you will find the list of unsupported features and services for Azure Arc-enabled SQL Managed Instance.

A feature of Azure Arc-enabled SQL Managed Instance is that it is *always current.* (You may also see the term "evergreen SQL" used.) Similar to the always current or evergreen SQL offerings available in Azure PaaS Services such as Azure SQL Managed Instance in Azure Cloud-hosted deployments, Microsoft will continuously publish updated SQL Managed Instance container images to the Microsoft Container Registry for Azure Arc-enabled SQL Managed Instance. Then, based on update policies defined in your deployment, you can specify how often and when the updates are applied to your environment. In traditional implementations of SQL Server, managing updates is a challenging and time-consuming process. Kubernetes provides the ability to absorb updates and change quickly and roll it out into the Cluster. This is the updated model used in Azure Arc-enabled Data Services.

Azure Arc-enabled SQL Managed Instance comes in two service tiers, General Purpose and Business Critical. As defined in Microsoft's documentation, General Purpose is a budget-friendly tier designed for most workloads with basic performance and availability. The Business-Critical tier is designed for performance-sensitive workloads with higher-availability requirements.

The General-Purpose service tier is now generally available. Its SQL Server feature set is the same as the standard edition with limitations on the number of cores and the amount of addressable memory an Azure Arc-enabled SQL Managed Instance can use – a maximum of up 24 CPU cores and 128GB of memory. This also this leads us to the next key point about Azure Arc-enabled SQL Managed Instance, *high availability.* In the General-Purpose service tier, Azure Arc-enabled SQL Managed Instance is deployed as a single SQL Server instance running in a Pod controlled by a StatefulSet. As discussed previously, a StatefulSet provides basic failover capabilities in an application or Node failure event. If there is a failure, the previous Pod is deleted, and a new Pod is created in its place. The recovery time for these failure scenarios can be very short.

Tip   When a Pod running SQL Server Managed Instance is created, it must run crash recovery on startup. Consider using Accelerated Data Recovery to reduce SQL Server Managed Instance startup time. For more details, go to *https://docs.microsoft.com/en-us/sql/relational-databases/ accelerated-database-recovery-concepts*.

To ensure high availability in this single-instance implementation, external, shared storage should be used and made available to all Nodes in the Cluster. In the event of a Node failure, they can be started elsewhere in the Cluster, and the Persistent Volume can then be mounted and made available to the new Pod.

Azure Arc-enabled SQL Managed Instance uses Kubernetes Services for a persistent access endpoint. As highlighted in Figure 2-7, applications and users that need access to the SQL Managed Instance deployed in Kubernetes will point to the IP or DNS Name and the defined Port for access into the database instance. This Service is independent of the life cycle of the Pod, and if the Pod dies and is created again elsewhere in the Cluster, the Service is updated and will send the traffic to the new Pod automatically.

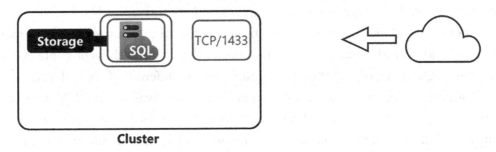

Cluster

Figure 2-7. A typical deployment of an Azure Arc-enabled SQL Managed Instance running in a Kubernetes Cluster

In Kubernetes, when you update a container image or make a Pod configuration change, the current Pods are deleted and new Pods are created using the updated container image or updated configuration. This is a very quick operation, but this can result in a small downtime, which may be unacceptable in some scenarios. In Azure Arc-enabled Data Services, the data services deployed are updated using this same model, so there is a small period of downtime when an update is rolled out for a deployed data service.

The Business-Critical service tier as shown in Figure 2-8 provides the SQL Server feature set of the enterprise edition with OS limits for the number of cores and the amount of addressable memory. In this service tier, high availability is provided by an Availability Group, where there are replicated copies of databases across multiple Nodes in the Kubernetes Cluster. The downtime is limited to the duration of the failover. Further, this Availability Group can be used for read scale-out operations.

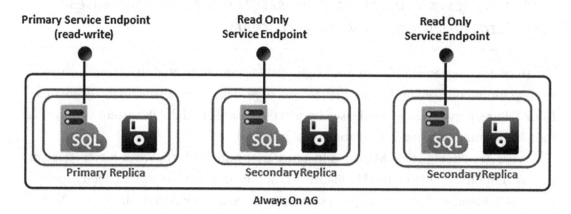

Figure 2-8. *Business-Critical service tier: collocated compute and storage*

For more information on the service tiers, please see this link: *https://docs. microsoft.com/en-us/azure/azure-arc/data/service-tiers*.

A benefit of the cloud is *elastic scale* enabling you to add capacity to an environment on demand and take advantage of that additional capacity as quickly as possible. Azure Arc-enabled SQL Managed Instance deployments are no different. If needed, you can add additional compute and memory capacity to a deployment of SQL Managed Instance by adjusting the assigned CPU and memory resources assigned to that deployment. Further, using the basic high-availability constructs of Kubernetes, this change is rolled out nearly immediately. The deployment is updated, and it creates a new Pod with this new configuration, and the SQL Managed Instance can use this additional scale-up capacity.

Azure Arc-enabled PostgreSQL Hyperscale

The second Azure Arc-enabled Data Service we want to introduce to you is *Azure Arc-enabled PostgreSQL Hyperscale*. Azure Arc-enabled PostgreSQL Hyperscale is a leading open source database used as a data store for mission-critical applications. PostgreSQL Hyperscale is an implementation in the Azure Cloud that enables you to horizontally scale data by sharding it across multiple instances and allows for distributed parallel query execution. A key element of Hyperscale's success is that it works with existing versions of Postgres database, so databases and their applications can use these benefits with little to no changes.

Azure Arc-enabled PostgreSQL Hyperscale also uses the *always current* or evergreen SQL model described in the previous section. Microsoft will continuously update the container image for PostgreSQL Hyperscale, and you can decide how often and when that image is rolled out into your environment.

As mentioned previously, a vital benefit of the cloud is *elastic scale*, being able to add capacity to your environment on demand and being able to take advantage of that additional capacity as quickly as possible. Azure Arc-enabled PostgreSQL Hyperscale highlights this elastic scale since it can scale out in terms of the number of Postgres Worker Nodes supporting the database and also shard the data across those Worker Nodes and their underlying storage. This enables both parallel query execution and also distributed I/O which can increase database capacity and performance.

Note   We want to call out that there is an overlap in terms used. A Postgres Worker Node is an individual compute unit in a Hyperscale Server Group. This is not the same as a Kubernetes Node, a compute resource in a Kubernetes Cluster.

When executing a scaling operation in Azure Arc-enabled PostgreSQL, additional Postgres Worker Nodes are added to the pool of Postgres Worker Nodes supporting the PostgreSQL Hyperscale Server Group. In Figure 2-9, you will see a PostgreSQL Hyperscale Server Group scaled from two Worker Nodes to three Worker Nodes. The data is then rebalanced across the three Worker Nodes in the Server Group. Scaling out is an online operation, and the sharded data is automatically rebalanced across the Worker Nodes in the current Server Group.

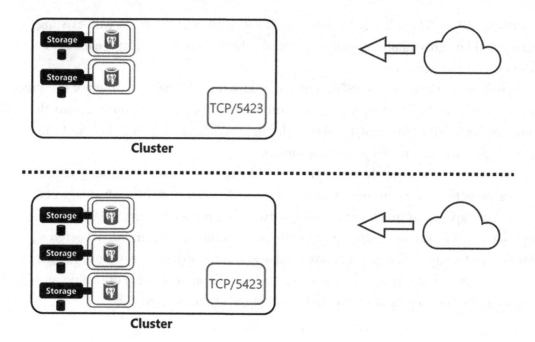

Figure 2-9. *A PostgreSQL Hyperscale Server Group scaled from two Worker Nodes to three Worker Nodes and data being rebalanced across the Worker Nodes*

In addition to scale-out, you can also scale up individual Postgres Worker Nodes by adding CPU and memory capacity to the deployments. Doing this will cause the Pods supporting the Postgres Workers to be restarted due to the new Pod configuration. At the time of this publication, scale-back operations are not supported. If you need to scale down, you can create a new instance, back up the data in the old instance, and restore it into the new instance. For more information on data placement and sharding data, check out *https://docs.microsoft.com/en-us/azure/azure-arc/data/concepts-distributed-postgres-hyperscale*.

Deployment Sizing Considerations

Azure Arc-enabled Data Services are deployed on Kubernetes. Kubernetes provides an abstraction over the hardware available in your on-premises data center or cloud. In this section, we want to introduce you to sizing considerations when designing your Azure Arc-enabled Data Services and the supporting Kubernetes Cluster. The specific topics we are going to cover are *compute* and *storage*. First up, let's look at compute.

Compute

Each Node in a Kubernetes Cluster contributes both CPU and memory capacity to the collection of overall available resources that can be allocated workloads deployed in the Cluster. The number and size of the Nodes deployed is a function of the required capacity needed to run the workload deployed in the Cluster and also any Cluster system functions. If additional capacity is required in a Cluster, the additional Nodes can be added, contributing to more CPU and memory capacity allocated to workload. If needed, larger Nodes can be added or used to replace smaller Nodes increasing the overall capacity of the Cluster. This concept of adding additional capacity as needed is key to the elasticity of cloud-based architectures.

When deploying Azure Arc-enabled Data Services, several components contribute to the overall footprint of the resources required to run a Cluster and support deployed workloads. This includes the resources needed by the Arc Management Control Plane and the resources required by the actual data services workload deployed and potentially any other workload that is deployed in the Cluster. Let's look at each of these in more detail:

- **Arc Management Control Plane**: Consisting of the Data Controller, Metrics, and Logging Pods. Each one of these services consumes both CPU and memory in the Cluster. For more information on the required resources for each, check out *https://docs.microsoft. com/en-us/azure/azure-arc/data/sizing-guidance#data-controller-sizing-details*.

- **Data Services Workload**: Each instance of a data service deployed in the Cluster will consume some amount of CPU, memory, and disk. How much of each of those resources depends on the workload that is running in each of those data services. For more information on workload sizing and minimum requirements for each of the data services available, check out *https://docs.microsoft.com/en-us/azure/azure-arc/data/sizing-guidance*.

- **Kubernetes System Pods**: On each Node in a Kubernetes Cluster, there is a collection of system Pods and services which perform critical Cluster functions, each of which consumes some amount of system resources. Resources are reserved for critical operations, and in scenarios when resources are scarce, user Pods can be evicted from a Node. More information about Reserved Compute Resources is available on *https://kubernetes.io/docs/tasks/administer-cluster/reserve-compute-resources/*.

- **Other Workloads**: If your Cluster is not dedicated to data services, don't forget to take that workload into your sizing calculations.

After getting a feel for how much workload needs to be deployed in the Cluster, the next thing you will need to do is determine the size of your Cluster Nodes and the number of Cluster Nodes required to run your workload efficiently and with Node-level redundancy.

- **Individual Node Size**: When sizing Nodes, CPU and memory cannot be overallocated. For example, if your Nodes have two cores and 16GB of RAM, you cannot create a database instance that is four cores and 32GB of RAM. Kubernetes will not be able to start that Pod up. So, you have to add a larger Node or reduce the allocation to that Pod. Microsoft documentation recommends leaving at least 25% of available resources on each Node in the Cluster to allow for growth and redundancy.

- **High Availability**: When sizing a Cluster for the amount of resources needed, ensure that you are provisioning enough Nodes with enough resources collectively to allow for at least one Node to fail or for planned maintenance. For critical systems, it is recommended that customers have an N+2 model, where two Nodes can be offline, and the Cluster will still function with no performance degradation or interruption in workload. On a Node failure, Pods running on the failed Node are moved onto the Cluster's remaining Nodes. There needs to be sufficient capacity for these Pods to run.

The key takeaway here is: ensure that you have enough Nodes to support the required amount of CPU and memory needed to run the desired workload in a Cluster even in the event of a Node failure. Further, make sure that an individual deployment of a data service does not require more resources than are available on a single Node in the Cluster. Otherwise, the Pods supporting that deployment will not be able to be started on a Node in the Cluster since no Nodes have enough resources to support that configuration. Further, you want to ensure that you leave at least 25% capacity available on each Node in the Cluster for growth and redundancy.

Storage

Now let's move on to planning for storage in Azure Arc-enabled Data Services Clusters. The amount of storage capacity and what type is needed depends on the workload being deployed. Fundamentally, the performance profile of a SQL Server instance running as a SQL Managed Instance in Arc-enabled Data Services is no different than you would see when SQL Server instance is deployed in any other platform, such as Azure or even on-premises. What is unique is how access to storage is configured and allocated to your data services workloads. Let's dig into each of those topics now.

As introduced earlier, in Kubernetes, storage is allocated dynamically from Storage Classes. When a data service instance, such as SQL Managed Instance or PostgreSQL Hyperscale, is deployed, you define which Storage Class you want to use for the different types of data in the deployment. Currently, the options available are *database data files*, *database backup files*, and *application log files* and, if using SQL Managed Instance, a location for the *database transaction log files*. If no Storage Class is specified when a data service instance is defined, the default Storage Class is used. Defining which Storage Class is used by which type of data is surfaced as a configuration parameter when defining an instance. This will be covered in much more detail later in the book.

When designing an Azure Arc-enabled Data Services Cluster, you will want to create Storage Classes that map back to the storage types needed in your Cluster based on the workload profile required. For example, you may need an individual Storage Class for each type of data in a data service instance such as database files, transaction log files, application log files, and backups. Each one of these Storage Classes potentially can map to a different storage subsystem, each having the required performance profile for that data being stored in that Storage Class.

Storage Classes can be configured to allocate storage from both local Node storage and remote shared storage. Local storage has the potential to be very fast if the high-speed disks are deployed inside the Node. But local Node storage provides no durability in the event of a Node failure. If a Node fails, then the data on that Node is at risk of data loss. A common pattern for using local Node storage is ensuring that the data in the applications using that type of storage is replicated between multiple Nodes for redundancy and availability. Replication combined with local high-speed disks is viable deployment option in some scenarios. Local storage is a viable option for the Business-Critical service tier which uses Availability Groups to replicate data between replicas.

When using remote shared storage, Nodes in the Cluster map storage from the remote storage system. This could be a SAN, NAS, or Cloud Files-based system. Provisioning storage using this architecture decouples the dependency of the local Node. If there is a Node failure, the Pod that was running on that Node can be scheduled onto another Node in the Cluster. The storage is mounted and exposed into the Pod, and the database instance can be back up and running quickly. The I/O interconnect from the Node to the shared storage environment should be provisioned with multiple paths for redundancy and also be of sufficient capacity to support the desired workload. Also, instances that require high I/O should be spread out across the Nodes in the Cluster using advanced Kubernetes scheduling techniques. For a deeper dive into storage and scheduling in Kubernetes, check out the Pluralsight course "Configuring and Managing Kubernetes Storage and Scheduling" at *www.pluralsight.com*.

Summary and Key Takeaways

This chapter introduced you to Azure Arc-enabled Data Services. It started with the challenges of modern hybrid cloud strategies. It then showed you how Azure Arc addresses those challenges to provide manageability at scale by extending the Azure Resource Manager to your on-premises or hybrid cloud environments. Next, we introduced the core Azure Arc-enabled resources, including Servers, Kubernetes, SQL Server, and Data Services. Then we dove deeper into what Azure Arc-enabled Data Services are, its architecture, how workloads are deployed and managed, and also discussed vital deployment considerations such as compute and storage capacity planning. In the next chapter, we will shift from theory into action and learn how to deploy an Arc Data Controller in a Kubernetes Cluster.

CHAPTER 3

Getting Ready for Deployment

In the previous chapter, we've talked about the theoretical concepts and components of Azure Arc-enabled Data Services.

Now it's time to get ready for a first deployment. Before we can get to the actual deployment of a Data Controller and subsequently database instances managed by that Data Controller, we do need some prerequisites as well as a Kubernetes Cluster in place. All these steps will guide you through what is necessary to start working with Azure Arc-enabled Data Services and make sure you're fully ready to go.

Note You will need an Azure account and subscription to complete these steps and to start a deployment. There are other deployment options available if Azure is not an option for you. Microsoft provides a Jumpstart site to make it easy to get going on-premises, in AWS, or Google's cloud. For more information, visit *https://azurearcjumpstart.io/*.

Prerequisites

Let us begin by looking at the prerequisites. While doing so, we'll point out some very useful helpers which – even though technically not necessary – will make our lives much easier. All the code that we'll be using here is available on this book's GitHub repository, and we're giving you the choice between deploying from a Linux and a Windows client depending on your preferences. We will not be going into details of an installation on MacOS, but the required tools including Azure Data Studio are available on this book's GitHub repository, too.

53

© Ben Weissman and Anthony E. Nocentino 2022
B. Weissman and A. E. Nocentino, *Azure Arc-enabled Data Services Revealed*,
https://doi.org/10.1007/978-1-4842-8085-0_3

Chocolatey

Before we get started, if you plan to deploy from a Windows client, we'd like to point your attention to Chocolatey or "choco." In case you haven't heard about it, choco is a free package manager for Windows which will allow us to install many of our prerequisites with a single line in PowerShell or a command prompt. Given that Windows Servers do not come with an easy-to-use built-in package manager, it just makes life much easier. You can find more information on *http://chocolatey.org* (see Figure 3-1), and you can even create an account and provide your own packages there.

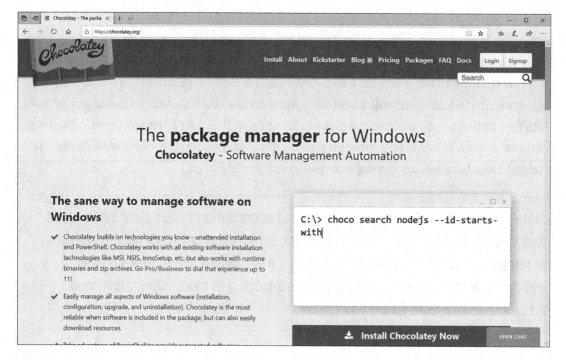

Figure 3-1. *Home page of Chocolatey*

From a simple user perspective though, there is no need to create an account or to download any installer.

To make choco available on your system, open a PowerShell window in administrative mode, and run the script shown in Listing 3-1.

Listing 3-1. Install Script for Chocolatey in PowerShell

```
[Net.ServicePointManager]::SecurityProtocol = [Net.ServicePointManager]::Se
curityProtocol -bor [Net.SecurityProtocolType]::Tls12
Set-ExecutionPolicy Bypass -Scope Process -Force; iex ((New-Object System.
Net.WebClient).DownloadString('https://chocolatey.org/install.ps1'))
```

Once the respective command has completed, choco is installed and ready to be used.

Tools on Windows

Let us start with a few little helpers that come with Linux by default, but are either missing or limited on Windows by default. By running the code in Listing 3-2, we'll install *curl* (to interact with websites), *grep* (to filter output on the command line), and *putty* (which also comes with *pscp*, a tool that will allow us to copy data from a Linux machine).

Listing 3-2. Install script for recommended tools

```
choco install curl -y
choco install grep -y
choco install putty -y
```

The first official prerequisite is the *kubernetes-cli,* which can be installed through the command in Listing 3-3.

Listing 3-3. Install script for kubectl

```
choco install kubernetes-cli -y
```

The last official requirement is the Azure command-line interface, which can also be installed through choco as shown in Listing 3-4.

Listing 3-4. Install script for the azure-cli

```
choco install azure-cli -y
```

That's it already for the official prerequisites. Despite that, we'll also install Azure Data Studio through the code in Listing 3-5, which will allow us to try out the graphical deployment experience.

Listing 3-5. Install script for Azure Data Studio

```
choco install azure-data-studio -y
```

Finally, let's create a directory and download a backup file of the AdventureWorks2017 database so we have something to restore later using the commands in Listing 3-6.

Listing 3-6. Download script for AdventureWorks2017

```
mkdir C:\Files
curl -L -o C:\Files\AdventureWorks2017.bak https://github.com/Microsoft/
sql-server-samples/releases/download/adventureworks/AdventureWorks2017.bak
```

Depending on the platform that you'll be deploying to, some of these tools may not be required. Given that they're all rather lightweight, we'd recommend installing them all anyway.

Tools on Ubuntu

If you prefer to deploy from an Ubuntu machine, you can do this using Ubuntu 18.04 or Ubuntu 20.04. Ubuntu comes with its own package manager (*apt*), so there is no need for Chocolatey or something similar. Before we can install the prerequisites though, we need to make the Microsoft repository a trusted source using the code in Listing 3-7.

Listing 3-7. apt script for basic prerequisites

```
sudo apt-get update
sudo apt-get install gnupg ca-certificates curl wget software-properties-
common apt-transport-https lsb-release -y
curl -sL https://packages.microsoft.com/keys/microsoft.asc |
gpg --dearmor |
sudo tee /etc/apt/trusted.gpg.d/microsoft.asc.gpg > /dev/null
```

Should you be using Ubuntu 18.04, run the code in Listing 3-8 to add the Microsoft repository to the list of known sources for package installations.

Listing 3-8. apt script to add Microsoft repository (Ubuntu 18.04)

```
AZ_REPO=$(lsb_release -cs)
echo "deb [arch=amd64] https://packages.microsoft.com/repos/azure-cli/
$AZ_REPO main" |
    sudo tee /etc/apt/sources.list.d/azure-cli.list
sudo apt-get update
```

Now we're ready to go ahead and install the Azure command-line interface and *kubectl* using the code from Listing 3-9.

Listing 3-9. apt script for azure-cli and kubectl

```
sudo apt-get install -y azure-cli
sudo apt-get install -y kubectl
```

That's it – your Ubuntu machine is ready to go to start a deployment.

If you want to use Azure Data Studio on Ubuntu as well, please follow the instructions at *https://docs.microsoft.com/en-us/sql/azure-data-studio/ download-azure-data-studio*.

Getting Azure Data Studio Ready

One of the big strengths of Azure Data Studio is its extensibility, which makes it super flexible and lightweight at the same time. This, on the other hand, means that we'll need to add and enable some extensions and configurations before we can use it for Azure Arc-enabled Data Services. While this could mostly be done "on the fly," we'd suggest getting everything in place so we can purely focus on the deployment afterward.

The first step is to install the Azure Arc extension. To do so, navigate to the extensions tab as shown in Figure 3-2.

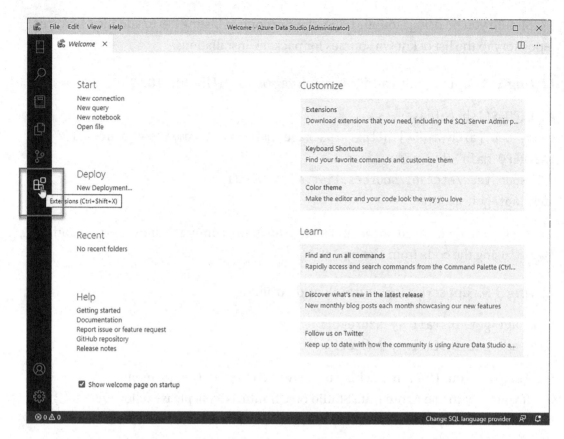

Figure 3-2. *Azure Data Studio – add extension*

In the extensions tab, search for "arc" and click install as shown in Figure 3-3.

Figure 3-3. *Azure Arc Extension Installation*

> **Note** If you plan to use Azure Data Studio with Postgres, now might be a good time to also install the Postgres extension. Just search for "postgres" in the extensions tab like you've searched for "arc," and it will show up.

Next, we need to add an Azure account to Azure Data Studio. To do so, navigate to the connections tab, expand the AZURE section, and select "Sign in to Azure…" as shown in Figure 3-4.

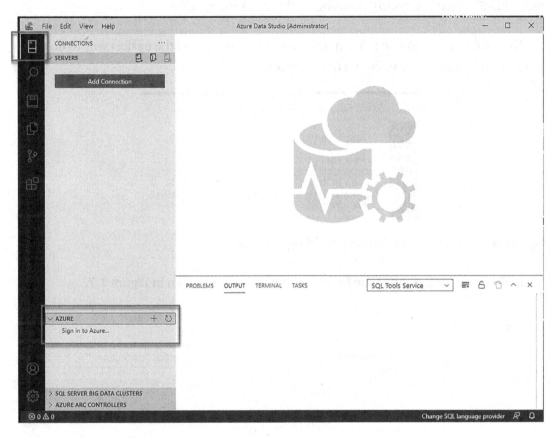

Figure 3-4. *Azure Data Studio – add connection*

This will trigger a login dialog which will, after successfully signing in, confirm that your account was added. Your Azure account should also show up in the linked accounts section in Azure Data Studio as shown in Figure 3-5.

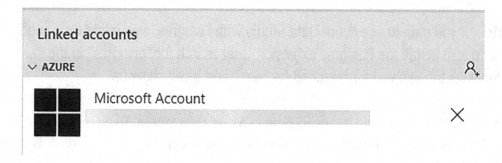

Figure 3-5. *Azure Account showing in Azure Data Studio*

Next, we need to enable Python in Azure Data Studio, and the easiest way to do so is to open a new notebook as shown in Figure 3-6.

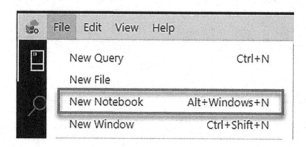

Figure 3-6. *Azure Data Studio – adding notebook*

In this notebook, change the Kernel to "Python 3" as shown in Figure 3-7.

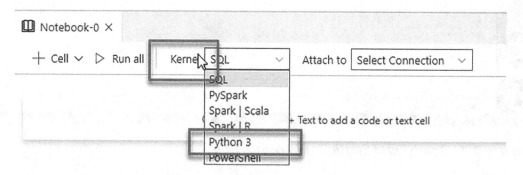

Figure 3-7. *Azure Data Studio - changing the kernel*

This will trigger the Python runtime configuration. We suggest a new python installation as also suggested by the wizard shown in Figure 3-8.

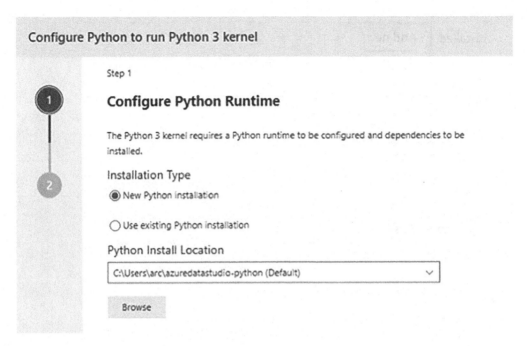

Figure 3-8. *Configure Python in ADS*

The installation can take a few minutes; once it has finished, you can see the kernel of the notebook showing as "Python 3" (see Figure 3-9).

Figure 3-9. *Azure Data Studio – kernel*

The last step is to install the "pandas" package. Navigate to the python packages by clicking the icon highlighted in Figure 3-10.

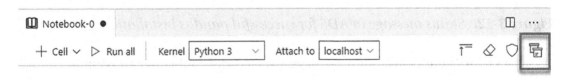

Figure 3-10. *Azure Data Studio – installing pandas package*

In the "Manage Packages" tab, switch to "Add new," search for pandas, and click "Install" as illustrated in Figure 3-11.

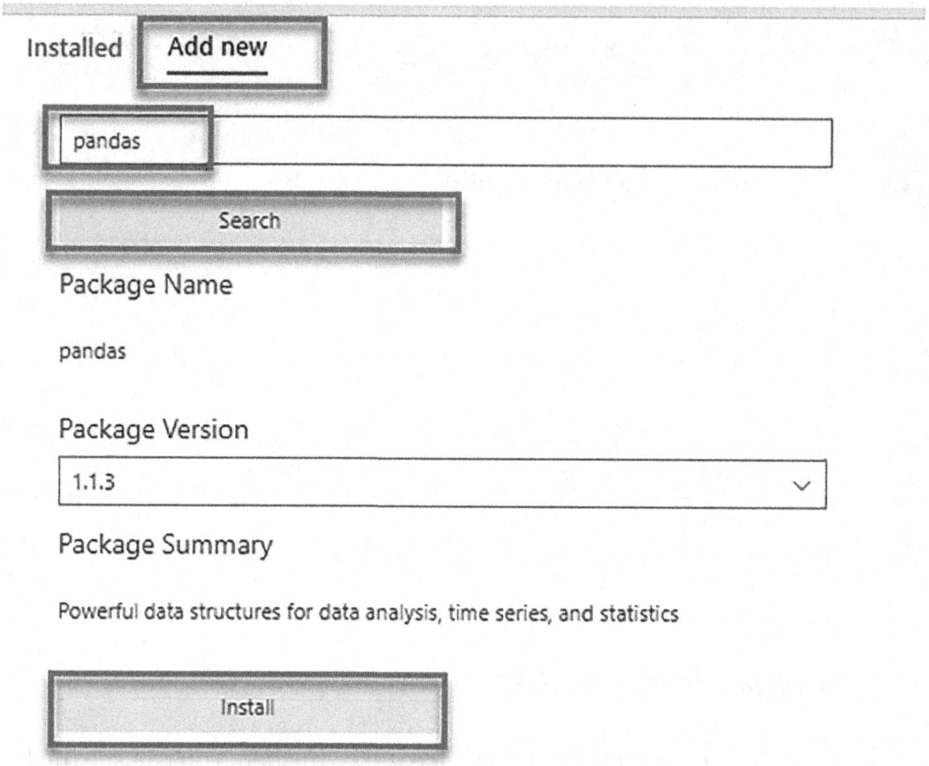

Installed | **Add new**

pandas

Search

Package Name

pandas

Package Version

1.1.3   ∨

Package Summary

Powerful data structures for data analysis, time series, and statistics

Install

Figure 3-11. *Azure Data Studio – managing packages*

You may close this wizard. The installation status will show and confirm when it's done (see Figure 3-12).

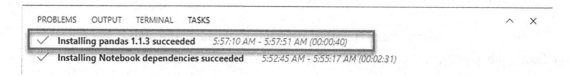

Figure 3-12. *Status message in ADS for successful pandas installation*

That's it for Azure Data Studio – we have installed and configured everything we'll need.

azure-cli Extensions and Providers

The azure-cli, which is the central tool for most deployments as we'll see in the upcoming chapters, requires a few extensions and registered providers to fully support the deployment of Azure Arc-enabled Data Services.

Those can be added/installed through the CLI itself using the code from Listing 3-10.

Listing 3-10. Command to install the required extensions and providers for the azure-cli

```
az extension add --name connectedk8s
az extension add --name k8s-extension
az extension add --name customlocation
az extension add --name arcdata
az provider register -n Microsoft.Kubernetes
az provider register -n Microsoft.KubernetesConfiguration
az provider register -n Microsoft.ExtendedLocation
```

Note   If you had installed any of these tools or extensions before, please make sure to upgrade them to the latest versions before proceeding.

Have a Resource Group in Azure

In Azure, we'll need a resource group to start with. This resource group will later be used to store your Logs and Metrics when uploading them to the Azure Portal (see Chapter 7). You can either create this through the Portal or by simply running the command in Listing 3-11.

Listing 3-11. azure-cli code to log in

```
az login
```

This command will open a web browser asking you to sign into your Azure account. Once you've signed in, the website will confirm this, the browser can be closed, and your azure-cli session is now authenticated. In case you have multiple subscriptions, make sure to set the context to the correct subscription ID using the command from Listing 3-12.

Listing 3-12. azure-cli code to set the current subscription context

```
az account set -s <Subscription>
```

To create the resource group, run the code from Listing 3-13, replacing the group name and location with suitable values for you. We will be using arcBook as our group's name and EastUS as our location throughout this book.

Listing 3-13. azure-cli code to create a resource group

```
az group create --name <groupname> --location <location>
```

Figure 3-13 is showing how the azure-cli will confirm the creation of this resource group.

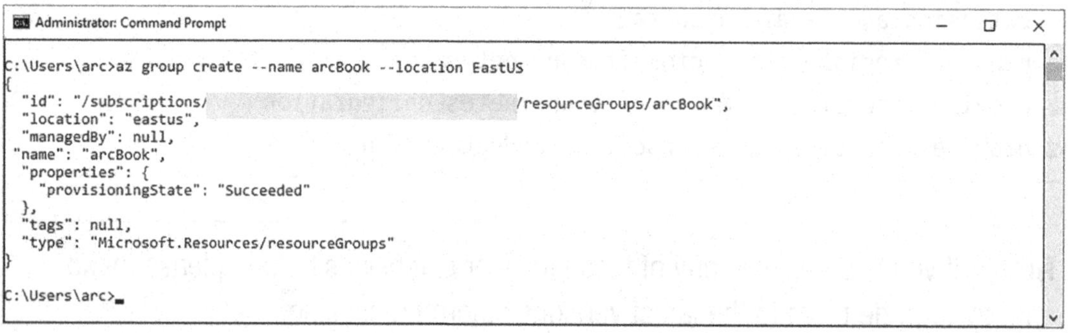

```
Administrator: Command Prompt                                              —   □   ×
C:\Users\arc>az group create --name arcBook --location EastUS
{
  "id": "/subscriptions/                              /resourceGroups/arcBook",
  "location": "eastus",
  "managedBy": null,
"name": "arcBook",
  "properties": {
    "provisioningState": "Succeeded"
  },
  "tags": null,
  "type": "Microsoft.Resources/resourceGroups"
}

C:\Users\arc>_
```

Figure 3-13. *Resource group creation confirmation*

As we've just created an empty resource group so far, this is not resulting in any charges in Azure yet.

Summary and Key Takeaways

In this chapter, we've guided you through the requirements to be fulfilled before starting a deployment of Arc-enabled Data Services. Now that you're ready, the only thing that's missing before we can really get started is a Kubernetes Cluster.

Installing Kubernetes

Given that – apart from the hardware – Kubernetes is the base layer of every Azure Arc-enabled Data Services deployment, you will need at least one Kubernetes Cluster to deploy to. Without going into too much detail, we will be showing you how to deploy a Cluster using a kubeadm (a self-installed Kubernetes flavor running on Linux). This is not the only option (see Chapter 2 for a list of supported options). The whole idea of Azure Arc-enabled Data Services is to be able to deploy services to any infrastructure in any cloud – but we want to provide you an easy option to get started. The deployment process explained in the following chapters is the same regardless of which target platform you choose.

This chapter will introduce how to build a Kubernetes Cluster on-premises using virtual machines. We will begin with a discussion of the decision process of where to install, on-premises or in the cloud, and what to consider in that process. We will then go through building an on-premises, virtual machine-based Kubernetes Cluster using the *kubeadm* installation method. This Cluster will be the foundation for all examples in the remainder of the book.

Installation Considerations and Methods

As with pretty much any modern software installation, the first thing you need to decide is: Will you be installing on-premises or to a cloud?

© Ben Weissman and Anthony E. Nocentino 2022
B. Weissman and A. E. Nocentino, *Azure Arc-enabled Data Services Revealed*,
https://doi.org/10.1007/978-1-4842-8085-0_4

Where to Deploy?

When deploying to a cloud, you need to choose between two major deployment options:

- **Infrastructure as a Service (IaaS)**: In an IaaS scenario, you're deploying *virtual machines* within your cloud and then installing Kubernetes on top of that.

- **Platform as a Service (PaaS)**: Kubernetes is also available as a managed service from all the big cloud providers. In a managed service offering, you don't have to worry about any of the underlying infrastructure or redundancy. The cloud provider handles that for you. One thing to consider with PaaS is that you will lose some flexibility in versioning and other features available inside Kubernetes and the access to the Control Plane Nodes. When deploying on-premises, the decision comes down to installing on virtual machines or directly on *bare metal*. While there are managed offerings available on-premises, those are out of the scope of this book.

The decision between bare metal and virtual machines as your Nodes mainly depends on your anticipated workload. If you're talking about many scalable microservices, Kubernetes Nodes running on VMs will probably give you a lot of extra flexibility. If you're deploying one single large application, the hypervisor in between will require unnecessary overhead. You may be wondering: If you're only running a single application, is Kubernetes even the best platform for this? As so often, the answer is: it depends! While they often warrant dedicated infrastructure, they only deploy on Kubernetes.

In this book, we will be focusing on an environment using self-managed (on-premises or cloud-based Infrastructure-as-a-Service) virtual machines. It doesn't matter if you installed those machines as VMs in the cloud, on-premises, or on bare metal, as Kubernetes abstracts the infrastructure away.

Going forward, looking at where to install a potential production Cluster, that question should follow your organization's general strategy. If all you do so far is still on-premises, it might make perfect sense for your Kubernetes Cluster to live there. If, on the other hand, you're in the process of or already have migrated significant workloads to the cloud, your Kubernetes Cluster probably should follow. In the end, this comes down to your team's skill set and the requirements of your use cases to run on Kubernetes.

Further Considerations

Besides the *where* question, there are, of course, other considerations of which we'll be talking about in more depth throughout this chapter and the remainder of the book:

- How many Worker Nodes do you need to support your workload?

- What's the CPU and RAM configuration of those Nodes?

- Do you need a highly available solution in case the Control Plane fails?

- What is your backup and restore strategy?

- What kind of storage(s) are you going to use?

- How are you going to manage networking between Pods and Nodes?

While we're at the beginning of your Kubernetes journey, those are all questions that you should have an answer to before considering a rollout of a production system.

Installation Methods

Depending on where you're installing, this will also, for the most part, determine your installation method. When installing a self-managed Cluster, you can choose mainly between kubeadm, which is a free and open source way of deploying Kubernetes on *Linux,* and enterprise offerings like RedHat OpenShift. The installation itself is usually triggered through command-line tools.

When installing a cloud-based Cluster, your cloud provider will take care of the installation part with the exact details behind the scenes being determined by your cloud provider. They usually offer their own command-line-based approaches and web portals for a guided deployment.

Additional Options

There are many additional options like using *Docker* Desktop to spin up a Kubernetes Cluster on your laptop or using lightweight hardware like a Raspberry Pi as your deployment target. While they may have valid use cases, especially in non-production environments, we will not go into depth on these in this book.

Also, while there are options to use Windows-based Worker Nodes, we will be focusing on using Linux as our operating system.

We also will not be going through the details of deploying a Single Node Cluster. If you only have a single *Ubuntu* machine available, you can use the code in Listing 4-1. This code will spin up a Single Node Cluster, including *local-storage,* but this will not be sufficient for most of the exercises in this book, except for the most basic ones.

Listing 4-1. Install Single Node Cluster

```
wget -q -O deploy_kubeadm.sh https://bookmark.ws/ArcDemo_Linux
chmod +x deploy_kubeadm.sh
./deploy_kubeadm.sh
```

Installation Requirements

For a self-managed Kubernetes installation, we will be focusing on kubeadm on Linux, more specifically Ubuntu. While CentOS, RHEL, and other Linux distributions are also supported, we just had to decide on one environment, and Ubuntu seems to be the most common choice these days.

The bare minimum system requirements are a system with two CPUs, 2GB of RAM, and swap disabled. These are the minimum requirements for a Kubernetes cluster to run, not accounting for the workloads running on the Cluster. In a production environment, you must ensure that you have accounted for your workload deployed and the scalability and redundancy.

In addition to those base system requirements, you'll also need a CRI (Container Runtime Interface) container runtime. The de facto standard is *containerd*. As Docker has been deprecated in Kubernetes 1.20 and its support has been removed in Kubernetes version 1.23, we will mainly focus on containerd in this book.

Network Requirements

From a networking perspective, make sure that all machines have unique hostnames, MAC addresses, and IP addresses. Those IP addresses should ideally be on the same subnet, but at the very least, must be set up to reach each other.

If you are running a firewall within your network (for the labs in this book, we recommend not to run a firewall, simply to avoid running into unnecessary complications with the network), Table 4-1 lists all the TCP Ports that need to be reachable on the Control Plane.

Table 4-1. *Required TCP Ports on Control Plane Node*

Component	TCP Port(s)
API	6443
etcd	2379-2380
Scheduler	10251
Controller Manager	10252
Kubelet	10250

The ports listed in Table 4-2 need to be open on the Nodes in your Cluster.

Table 4-2. *Required TCP Ports on Worker Nodes*

Component	TCP Port(s)
Kubelet	10250
NodePort	30000-32767

Note   The TCP Ports listed here are the default ports. In case you changed those, adjust your firewall rules accordingly.

Getting Kubernetes

Of course, to install Kubernetes, we need to get Kubernetes. The Kubernetes software is maintained on GitHub, so if you go to *https://GitHub.com/Kubernetes/Kubernetes/*, you will find the Kubernetes project. You can also contribute your ideas and changes to the project. This is also a precious resource to understand, in detail, how things work since you can view the code and learn from other people's experiences with GitHub issues.

In addition to the software itself, this is also where you will find additional documentation.

While, in theory, you could get the code and compile everything on your own, we'll make our lives a bit easier and install Kubernetes through a package manager.

Building a Self-Managed Cluster

With that theory in place, let's start working on building our first Kubernetes Cluster running on Ubuntu machines using kubeadm. We will be using the environment as described in Chapter 1, including the prerequisites mentioned there.

Virtual Machine-Based Kubernetes Cluster Requirements

We will need some compute and storage resources for the Kubernetes Clusters we will build in this chapter. For our lab, we will use a set of four Linux virtual machines. The minimum requirement to deploy a Data Controller is four cores, plus additional cores for any workload deployed. For the labs in this book, each virtual machine will need 8 vCPUs, 16GB of RAM, and 150GB of disk space, running Ubuntu Server 18.04 as an operating system. We have tested the code in this book on Ubuntu 18.04. Kubernetes is supported on several operating systems. Check out *https://kubernetes.io/docs/ setup/production-environment/tools/kubeadm/install-kubeadm/* for more details.

Note   The system resources provisioned here, 8 vCPUs and 16GB of RAM, are the bare minimum needed to bootstrap an Azure Arc-enabled Data Services Controller and Data Services such as SQL Managed Instance and Postgres. You will need additional resources based on the workload you want to run in your data service instances. If you are memory constrained when provisioning data service instances in the examples throughout the book, you may consider deleting the data service instances once you complete an exercise.

Getting the VMs Ready

After you've created the virtual machines needed for the lab in this book, it's time to discuss the networking configuration for those virtual machines.

Virtual Machine Network Configuration

Configure the lab VMs' IP addresses as specified in Table 4-3. You can use different IP addresses in your lab, but you will need to account for that in several of the labs when building your Cluster.

Table 4-3. *Virtual Machine Configuration*

Name	IP Address	Function
control	172.16.94.10	Control Plane Node
node-1	172.16.94.11	Worker Node
node-2	172.16.94.12	Worker Node
node-3	172.16.94.13	Worker Node
workstation (optional)	172.16.94.100	Administrative workstation (Windows)

Next, in IT, there's a saying, it's always DNS. In an enterprise environment, you can work with your networking team to provision the DNS entries defined earlier. For our lab, we will add host entries to the /etc/hosts file on each of these systems to ensure we can address all of the systems by name in our lab. In Listing 4-2, you will find the contents of our /etc/hosts file. Your hosts file may have entries for localhost and possibly other configurations.

Listing 4-2. Required additional Linux hosts file contents

```
172.16.94.10    control
172.16.94.11    node-1
172.16.94.12    node-2
172.16.94.13    node-3
```

On a Windows machine, you will find the file under *C:\Windows\System32\ drivers\ etc\hosts.*

Note   To edit the hosts file on Windows, make sure to run your editor as administrator.

Before moving on, please be sure that you have console or SSH access (by using the hostname) to all these virtual machines and that they can connect to each other over your network.

Note   All our scripts use the hostnames/IP addresses described earlier. If you build your lab using different settings, you will need to adjust the scripts used in the book accordingly. We'll not be pointing out every instance where this may be required individually for readability purposes.

System Swap Settings

As our last step, let's ensure that swap is disabled on our Control Plane Node and the three Worker Nodes, as this is a requirement of the kubelet.

Open an individual SSH connection into each virtual machine, and remove any swap partitions from */etc/fstab* using your favorite text editor. Next, run the command in Listing 4-3, which will also use sed to comment out the swap entry in your system's /etc/fstab.

If no output is returned, then your swap is disabled. You should reboot your virtual machine to ensure the setting persists on reboot.

Listing 4-3.   Disable swap

```
swapoff -a
sudo sed -i '/swap/s/^\(.*\)$/#\1/g' /etc/fstab
```

Software Package Installation

Next, we need to install both containerd and the Kubernetes packages on all virtual machines as described in the following two paragraphs. Unless mentioned otherwise, just run the commands as stated using a shell on each virtual machine.

Installing and Configuring containerd

To install containerd, we need to load two modules (*overlay* and *br_netfilter*) using the code in Listing 4-4. They are required by the OverlayFS used by the container runtime and for networking inside the Cluster.

Listing 4-4. Install modprobe and br_netfilter

```
sudo modprobe overlay
sudo modprobe br_netfilter
```

Using the code in Listing 4-5, we need to make sure those are also loaded on reboot.

Listing 4-5. Persist modprobe and br_netfilter

```
cat <<EOF | sudo tee /etc/modules-load.d/containerd.conf
overlay
br_netfilter
EOF
```

containerd also requires a few system parameters which we can set and persist using the command in Listing 4-6.

Listing 4-6. Persist system parameters for containerd

```
cat <<EOF | sudo tee /etc/sysctl.d/99-kubernetes-cri.conf
net.bridge.bridge-nf-call-iptables  = 1
net.ipv4.ip_forward                 = 1
net.bridge.bridge-nf-call-ip6tables = 1
EOF
```

Next, let's apply those settings without rebooting using the command in Listing 4-7.

Listing 4-7. Apply sysctl changes

```
sudo sysctl --system
```

Now our prerequisites for containerd are in place, so we can install it through *apt-get* as shown in Listing 4-8.

Listing 4-8. Install containerd

```
sudo apt-get update
sudo apt-get install -y containerd
```

containerd requires a configuration file, and we can use containerd itself to generate one with default settings (Listing 4-9).

Listing 4-9. Create containerd config

```
sudo mkdir -p /etc/containerd
sudo containerd config default | sudo tee /etc/containerd/config.toml
```

In this file, we must set the *cgroup driver* for containerd to *systemd* as this is required for the kubelet.

Open the file */etc/containerd/config.toml* in a text editor as root (e.g., through *vi* as shown in Listing 4-10).

Listing 4-10. Edit containerd config

```
sudo vi /etc/containerd/config.toml
```

In this file, find the section shown in Listing 4-11.

Listing 4-11. The configuration section in the containerd config file

```
[plugins."io.containerd.grpc.v1.cri".containerd.runtimes.runc]
```

Below that, look for the line SystemdCgroup = false and change the value from the default of false to true (as in Listing 4-12).

Listing 4-12. Lines to be edited in the containerd config file, change false to true

```
[plugins."io.containerd.grpc.v1.cri".containerd.runtimes.runc.options]
  ...
  SystemdCgroup = true
```

Note   Indentation matters here – this can be tabs or spaces! Make sure your file looks like the one in Figure 4-1!

```
[plugins."io.containerd.grpc.v1.cri".containerd.runtimes.runc.options]
    BinaryName = ""
    CriuImagePath = ""
    CriuPath = ""
    CriuWorkPath = ""
    IoGid = 0
    IoUid = 0
    NoNewKeyring = false
    NoPivotRoot = false
    Root = ""
    ShimCgroup = ""
    SystemdCgroup = true
```

Figure 4-1. *Indentation in containerd config file*

To exit vi and save the file, hit *ESC* and then type *:x!.*

Based on our new settings, we can use `systemctl` to restart containerd as shown in Listing 4-13.

Listing 4-13. Restart containerd

```
sudo systemctl restart containerd
```

containerd is now ready for use, and we can move on to installing the Kubernetes packages. You can confirm the status of the service using the command in Listing 4-14.

Listing 4-14. Status of containerd

```
sudo systemctl status containerd
```

Installing and Configuring Kubernetes Packages

As we will be installing packages from the Google Apt Repository, we will need to add Google's apt repository *gpg key* first (Listing 4-15).

Listing 4-15. Add Google gpg key

```
curl -s https://packages.cloud.google.com/apt/doc/apt-key.gpg | sudo apt-key add -
```

With that key in place, we next add the Kubernetes apt repository (Listing 4-16).

Listing 4-16. Add Kubernetes apt repository

```
sudo bash -c 'cat <<EOF >/etc/apt/sources.list.d/kubernetes.list
deb https://apt.kubernetes.io/ kubernetes-xenial main
EOF'
```

Let's update the apt package list and look at the available versions for the kubelet using the code in Listing 4-17.

Listing 4-17. Update apt package list

```
sudo apt-get update
apt-cache policy kubelet | head -n 20
```

This shows the available versions, and as you can see in Figure 4-2, at the time of writing, the latest available version is 1.20.4.

```
aen@control:~$ apt-cache policy kubelet | head -n 20
kubelet:
  Installed: (none)
  Candidate: 1.23.1-00
  Version table:
     1.23.1-00 500
        500 https://apt.kubernetes.io kubernetes-xenial/main amd64 Packages
     1.23.0-00 500
        500 https://apt.kubernetes.io kubernetes-xenial/main amd64 Packages
     1.22.5-00 500
        500 https://apt.kubernetes.io kubernetes-xenial/main amd64 Packages
     1.22.4-00 500
        500 https://apt.kubernetes.io kubernetes-xenial/main amd64 Packages
     1.22.3-00 500
        500 https://apt.kubernetes.io kubernetes-xenial/main amd64 Packages
     1.22.2-00 500
        500 https://apt.kubernetes.io kubernetes-xenial/main amd64 Packages
     1.22.1-00 500
        500 https://apt.kubernetes.io kubernetes-xenial/main amd64 Packages
     1.22.0-00 500
        500 https://apt.kubernetes.io kubernetes-xenial/main amd64 Packages
```

Figure 4-2. *Version list for kubelet*

We can now install kubelet, kubeadm, and kubectl as shown in Listing 4-18. If your current machine is also the one you've used to install kubectl in Chapter 1, you may get a message that it's already installed.

Listing 4-18. Install Kubernetes packages

```
sudo apt-get install -y kubelet kubeadm kubectl
```

This will install the latest version of each of these tools. Should you wish to install a previous version, you can specify that as shown in Listing 4-19.

Listing 4-19. Installing a specific version of Kubernetes packages

```
VERSION=1.22.4-00
sudo apt-get install -y kubelet=$VERSION kubeadm=$VERSION kubectl=$VERSION
```

To avoid automatic updates, we mark those tools (and containerd) as hold (Listing 4-20). This gives us full control over the patching process, running it independent from patching the base operating system.

Note   The code in this book is tested against Kubernetes version 1.22.4. Please monitor the Azure Arc-enabled Data Services release notes for supported Kubernetes versions by visiting *https://docs.microsoft.com/en-us/ azure/azure-arc/data/release-notes.*

Listing 4-20. Mark Kubernetes packages and containerd as hold

```
sudo apt-mark hold kubelet kubeadm kubectl containerd
```

Let's check the status of our kubelet and our container runtime (Listing 4-21).

Listing 4-21. Check the status of kubelet and containerd

```
sudo systemctl status kubelet.service
sudo systemctl status containerd.service
```

As you can see in Figure 4-3, the kubelet will enter a crashloop. This is normal behavior until a Cluster is created or the Node is joined to an existing Cluster (you can leave that process by hitting *q*).

```
aen@control:~$ sudo systemctl status kubelet.service
● kubelet.service - kubelet: The Kubernetes Node Agent
   Loaded: loaded (/lib/systemd/system/kubelet.service; enabled; vendor preset: enabled)
   Drop-In: /etc/systemd/system/kubelet.service.d
            └─10-kubeadm.conf
   Active: activating (auto-restart) (Result: exit-code) since Tue 2021-12-28 22:56:40 UTC; 9s ago
     Docs: https://kubernetes.io/docs/home/
  Process: 3540 ExecStart=/usr/bin/kubelet $KUBELET_KUBECONFIG_ARGS $KUBELET_CONFIG_ARGS $KUBELET_KUBEADM_ARGS $KUBELET_EXTRA_ARGS (code=exited, status=1/FAILURE)
 Main PID: 3540 (code=exited, status=1/FAILURE)
```

Figure 4-3. *Status of kubelet and containerd*

Also, make sure that both services are set to start when the system starts up. This can be set through the commands in Listing 4-22.

Listing 4-22. Enable startup on reboot for kubelet and containerd

```
sudo systemctl enable kubelet.service
sudo systemctl enable containerd.service
```

Note   Remember to repeat this process and install and configure these packages on each node, *control*, *node-1*, *node-2*, and *node-3*, individually!

Creating a Control Plane

With our container runtime and Kubernetes packages now in place, we can move on to create our Control Plane.

Note   All commands in this section need to be executed on your *control VM*.

Pod Networking

Before we initialize our Control Plane, we need to get the IP address that we will use for our Pod Network. For Pod Networking, there are many different solutions out there, and we have decided to keep it simple and use *Flannel*. While it doesn't have all the advanced configuration settings like *Calico*, another popular Pod Network, it works without any additional configuration on local and cloud networks, which tend to restrict *IPIP* packages, for example.

Download the default manifest using the *wget* command in Listing 4-23.

Listing 4-23. Download flannel

```
wget https://raw.githubusercontent.com/flannel-io/flannel/master/
Documentation/kube-flannel.yml
```

There are no required changes to the file, but inside that file defines the Pod CIDR IP range. Around line 128, you will find the network range defined. Listing 4-24 shows the code from the file. In the network field, you will find the value 10.244.0.0/16. This is the network range used to allocate IP addresses to Pods in the Cluster. We will not change this value in our lab. You may need to change this value in yours if the network overlaps with other IP ranges in your network environment.

Listing 4-24. Pod CIDR Network range in kube-flannel.yaml

```
net-conf.json: |
    {
      "Network": "10.244.0.0/16",
      "Backend": {
        "Type": "vxlan"
      }
    }
```

Bootstrapping Your Control Plane

We're ready to initialize our Cluster using kubeadm, as shown in Listing 4-25. Take note that we define the parameter --pod-network-cidr and set the value to the same value from the kube-flannel.yaml manifest. If you updated the value for your Pod Network, please edit that value here. We are using the default from the manifest.

Listing 4-25. Initialize Cluster

```
sudo kubeadm init --pod-network-cidr=10.244.0.0/16
```

Run this code on your control Node. This will take a few minutes and will output its progress constantly. When complete, the result should look like what you see in Figure 4-4.

```
Your Kubernetes control-plane has initialized successfully!

To start using your cluster, you need to run the following as a regular user:

  mkdir -p $HOME/.kube
  sudo cp -i /etc/kubernetes/admin.conf $HOME/.kube/config
  sudo chown $(id -u):$(id -g) $HOME/.kube/config

Alternatively, if you are the root user, you can run:

  export KUBECONFIG=/etc/kubernetes/admin.conf

You should now deploy a pod network to the cluster.
Run "kubectl apply -f [podnetwork].yaml" with one of the options listed at:
  https://kubernetes.io/docs/concepts/cluster-administration/addons/

Then you can join any number of worker nodes by running the following on each as root:

kubeadm join 172.16.94.10:6443 --token f1hmmg.nt8i4b7ea1nabiva \
        --discovery-token-ca-cert-hash sha256:7abbaee8d1577891aab3a6a72f9298331d1a6de7f5e168856abe32165729c17e
```

Figure 4-4.   The output of kubeadm init

To ensure that we can interact with our Cluster using a non-elevated shell, we need to create a kubeconfig file and store it in our home directory, as shown in Listing 4-26.

Listing 4-26.   Create kubectl configuration

```
mkdir -p $HOME/.kube
sudo cp -i /etc/kubernetes/admin.conf $HOME/.kube/config
sudo chown $(id -u):$(id -g) $HOME/.kube/config
```

Note   If you are using an administrative workstation, you can take this file and copy it or its contents to *.kube/config* in your home directory on this workstation. This will allow you to communicate with your Cluster from that workstation.

Deploying a Pod Network

Before joining our Worker Nodes, we need to ensure that our Pod Network is set up. As there are no required changes, we'll go straight ahead and install it using kubectl (Listing 4-27). We will be talking more about kubectl later in this chapter, so don't worry if this feels a bit unexplained at this point.

Listing 4-27. Install flannel

```
kubectl apply -f kube-flannel.yml
```

Your Pod Networking with Flannel is now set up.

Adding Nodes to a Cluster

Our Control Plane is ready, and our Pod Network is deployed, but we're not quite ready to join our Nodes yet. For a Node to be able to join a Cluster, we need a token. The easiest way is to generate a *join command* directly using kubeadm, as shown in Listing 4-28.

Listing 4-28. Generate token and join command

```
kubeadm token create --print-join-command
```

The output looks similar to what you see in Figure 4-5.

```
aen@control:~$ kubeadm token create --print-join-command
kubeadm join 172.16.94.10:6443 --token m87vj8.i1q0t7107jhg0upp --discovery-token-ca-cert-hash sha256:9df160ef427a69e12ca5d74bd6c22249975f26e72c6d048ba8d252d577786101
```

Figure 4-5. *Join command*

Now, we can take this command and run it (as root, see Listing 4-29) on each of our desired Worker Nodes, initiating the join process. Your join command will be different because the CA certificate is unique. The join token is a ticket valid for 24 hours, so if you want to add more Nodes later, you will need to create a new token.

Listing 4-29. kubeadm join command

```
sudo kubeadm join 172.16.94.10:6443 \
    --token m87vj8.i1q0t7107jhg0upp \
    --discovery-token-ca-cert-hash sha256:9df160ef427a69e12ca5d74bd
6c22249975f26e72c6d048ba8d252d577786101
```

Note   Make sure to add *sudo* – the command needs to be run as root, and the *--print-join-command* does not add it for you!

The Nodes will report that they have started the join process, as shown in Figure 4-6.

```
aen@node-1:~$ sudo kubeadm join 172.16.94.10:6443 --token m87vj8.i1q0t7107jhg0upp --discovery-token-ca-cert-hash sha256:9df160ef427a69e12ca5d74bd6c22249975f26e72c6d048ba8d252d577786101
[preflight] Running pre-flight checks
[preflight] Reading configuration from the cluster...
[preflight] FYI: You can look at this config file with 'kubectl -n kube-system get cm kubeadm-config -o yaml'
[kubelet-start] Writing kubelet configuration to file "/var/lib/kubelet/config.yaml"
[kubelet-start] Writing kubelet environment file with flags to file "/var/lib/kubelet/kubeadm-flags.env"
[kubelet-start] Starting the kubelet
[kubelet-start] Waiting for the kubelet to perform the TLS Bootstrap...

This node has joined the cluster:
* Certificate signing request was sent to apiserver and a response was received.
* The Kubelet was informed of the new secure connection details.

Run 'kubectl get nodes' on the control-plane to see this node join the cluster.
```

Figure 4-6. *Join command*

Let us list the Nodes by running kubectl on the Control Plane (see Listing 4-30).

Listing 4-30. List Nodes in Cluster

```
kubectl get nodes
```

If you run this command shortly after joining a Worker Node to the Cluster, you may find that Nodes are showing up but are *NotReady* yet (see Figure 4-7).

```
aen@control:~$ kubectl get nodes
NAME       STATUS     ROLES                  AGE     VERSION
control    Ready      control-plane,master   3m54s   v1.22.4
node-1     NotReady   <none>                 1s      v1.22.4
```

Figure 4-7. *Nodes in Cluster*

Nodes will show as *NotReady* because the Pods that run Pod Networking and kube-proxy are currently deploying. If you run the command again after a few minutes, the Nodes will show as *Ready*. You should not proceed forward until all your Nodes are joined to the Cluster and they each show as *Ready*, as in Figure 4-8.

```
aen@control:~$ kubectl get nodes
NAME       STATUS   ROLES                  AGE     VERSION
control    Ready    control-plane,master   9m12s   v1.22.4
node-1     Ready    <none>                 5m19s   v1.22.4
node-2     Ready    <none>                 4m18s   v1.22.4
node-3     Ready    <none>                 3m22s   v1.22.4
```

Figure 4-8. *All Nodes in Cluster showing Ready*

Provisioning Storage in Your Cluster

The focus of this book is Azure Arc-enabled Data Services and the Data Controller, and the data service instances deployed need access to persistent storage in the Cluster. For our lab environment in this book, we use the local storage available on each Node in the Cluster. While this is good for our lab scenario, this isn't the best choice for production workloads. You will want to use enterprise-class storage for your Clusters and application data. Let's dive into how to configure the dynamic provisioning of local storage for our lab Cluster.

First, on each Node in the Cluster, you will create a set of directories used as Persistent Volumes in your Cluster. In Listing 4-31, we define a loop that will create 80 directories used as Persistent Volumes. Pods scheduled to the Node with Persistent Volume Claims will have Persistent Volumes provisioned for these directories on that Node.

Listing 4-31. Creating directories for Persistent Volumes

```
for i in $(seq 1 80); do
  vol="vol$i"
  sudo mkdir -p /azurearc/local-storage/$vol
  sudo mount --bind /azurearc/local-storage/$vol /azurearc/local-
storage/$vol
done
```

Next, we will deploy the local storage provisioner. This provisioner is responsible for binding a Persistent Volume Claim to a Persistent Volume. The code to deploy the local storage provisioning is in Listing 4-32. This code creates a Storage Class named `local-storage`.

Listing 4-32. Creating the local storage provisioner

```
kubectl apply -f https://raw.githubusercontent.com/microsoft/sql-server-
samples/master/samples/features/azure-arc/deployment/kubeadm/ubuntu/local-
storage-provisioner.yaml
```

With the local provisioner created, the next step is to set that local storage provisioner as the default Storage Class in the Cluster. The code to set this as default is in Listing 4-33.

Listing 4-33. Setting the local-storage Storage Class as default

```
kubectl patch storageclass local-storage -p '{"metadata":
{"annotations":{"storageclass.kubernetes.io/is-default-class":"true"}}}'
```

With the local storage provisioner deployed in the Cluster, when we provision data service instances, you can specify a Storage Class. In all our examples in this book, we will use this local-storage Storage Class to provision storage. If you do not specify a Storage Class, the default Storage Class is used, and in our Cluster, that is the local-storage Storage Class.

Before proceeding, confirm that your Storage Class is configured and set as default. You can do that with the code in Listing 4-34, and you should have the same output as in Figure 4-9. Take note of the Storage Class name, which is `local-storage`, and that it is marked as default since the name is suffixed with (`default`).

Listing 4-34. Get a listing of Storage Classes in your Cluster

```
kubectl get storageclass
```

```
aen@control:~$ kubectl get storageclass
NAME                     PROVISIONER                     RECLAIMPOLICY   VOLUMEBINDINGMODE      ALLOWVOLUMEEXPANSION   AGE
local-storage (default)  kubernetes.io/no-provisioner    Delete          WaitForFirstConsumer   false                  30h
```

Figure 4-9. *A listing of the Storage Classes in our Cluster*

Accessing Your Cluster with kubectl

kubectl is the primary command-line tool for interacting with your Kubernetes Cluster. We've used kubectl several times in this chapter during the Cluster bootstrapping process and deploying our Pod Network, and we ran those commands while logged in locally on the Control Plane Node.

kubectl interacts with the API Server over HTTPS. This means you can access the API Server from over a network if the API Server is reachable from the client you're using, allowing you to interact with your Cluster over the network. In this section, we will rename our context to a more user-friendly name and then copy the kubeconfig file to both Windows and Linux machines for remote access to our Cluster. You will need to do these steps to perform some of the exercises in the book.

Renaming a kubeconfig Context

A kubeconfig Cluster context is a configuration entry in a kubeconfig file that defines a Cluster's network location, a username for authentication, and an authentication credential for your Cluster. You can have several Cluster contexts in a kubeconfig file. It is often helpful to name a Cluster context a meaningful name rather than keeping the default. So, let's do that together.

On your Control Plane Node, let's rename our existing kubeconfig context from the default of kubernetes-admin@kubernetes to something more meaningful. We will name this kubeconfig context to kubeadm to describe the Cluster we've created together in this chapter. kubeadm is the common term used to describe a kubeadm-based Cluster in Microsoft documentation and Azure Data Studio's Azure Arc-enabled Data Services and azure-cli deployment workflows. To rename a kubeconfig context, use the code in Listing 4-35.

Listing 4-35. Renaming a kubeconfig context

```
kubectl config rename-context kubernetes-admin@kubernetes kubeadm
```

In Figure 4-10, you will find the output of a successful context renaming.

```
aen@control:~$ kubectl config rename-context kubernetes-admin@kubernetes kubeadm
Context "kubernetes-admin@kubernetes" renamed to "kubeadm".
```

Figure 4-10. *A listing of the Cluster configuration contexts in our kubeconfig file*

With the Cluster context renamed, now let's copy that Cluster context to a Windows and Linux workstation for remote access to the Cluster.

From a Windows Workstation

You can copy the kubeconfig file from the Control Plane Node to the local Windows workstation using the pscp command. We installed pscp in Chapter 3 when we installed the putty package. In Listing 4-36, the code first creates a .kube directory in the current user's profile. Then it uses pscp to copy the kubeconfig file named config file from the home directory of the user you bootstrapped your Cluster with on the Control Plane Node to the user profile of the current user on the Windows workstation in a subdirectory .kube. Once copied there, kubectl can read that file for its Cluster context.

CHAPTER 4   INSTALLING KUBERNETES

Listing 4-36. Copying your kubeconfig file from the Control Node to your Windows workstation

```
mkdir %USERPROFILE%\.kube
pscp -P 22 <login>@control:/home/<login>/.kube/config %USERPROFILE%\.kube\
```

Note   Earlier in this chapter, as part of the Cluster bootstrapping process, you copied /etc/kubernetes/admin.conf to $HOME/.kube/config on the Control Plane Node. You are copying the config from this $HOME directory onto your Windows workstation.

Once you have copied your Cluster context to your Windows workstation, from that workstation, you will want to confirm that kubectl can use that file, and you can do that by getting the current Cluster context with the code from Listing 4-37, and the output should match the output shown in Figure 4-11.

Listing 4-37. Retrieve active Kubernetes context

```
kubectl config current-context
```

```
C:\>kubectl config current-context
kubeadm
```

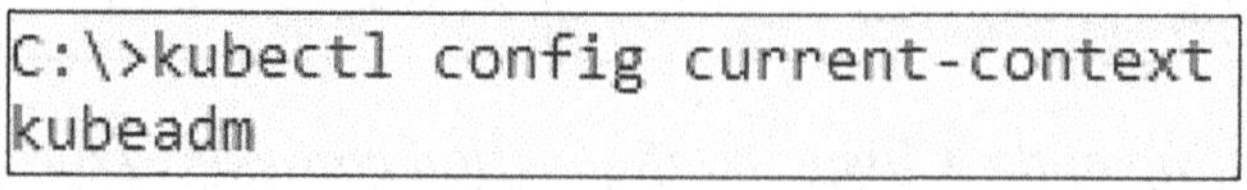

Figure 4-11. *A listing of the Cluster configuration contexts in our kubeconfig file on a Windows workstation*

Once you've confirmed kubectl is reading the correct kubeconfig file, you will want to test connectivity to your Cluster using the code in Listing 4-38.

Listing 4-38. Testing connectivity to your Cluster

```
kubectl cluster-info
```

Once executed, you should see output like in Figure 4-12. You can confirm that you are pointing at the right Kubernetes Cluster by looking at the Control Plane Node's URL, which in our lab environment is https://172.16.94.10:6443; that's the location of the API Server.

```
C:\>kubectl cluster-info
Kubernetes control plane is running at https://172.16.94.10:6443
CoreDNS is running at https://172.16.94.10:6443/api/v1/namespaces/kube-system/services/kube-dns:dns/proxy
```

Figure 4-12. *A listing of Cluster information. Confirming connectivity from our Windows client to the remote Cluster*

Now let's move forward and copy our kubeconfig file from the Control Plane Node to a Linux workstation.

From a Linux Workstation

To copy a kubeconfig file from your Control Plane Node to a Linux workstation, you can use the scp command natively installed on many Linux distributions. In Listing 4-39, you will find the copy to copy a kubeconfig file from the Control Plane Node to a remote Linux workstation. Log in to the Linux machine you want to copy the file to and run this code on that system.

Note   This code will overwrite your current kubeconfig file named *config*. You may want to save a backup of your existing kubeconfig file.

Listing 4-39. Copying your kubeconfig file from the Control Node to your Linux workstation

```
mkdir $HOME/.kube
scp aen@control:~/.kube/config $HOME/.kube/config
```

Like in the preceding Windows example, please use kubectl config current-context to ensure you have the Cluster context configured properly and use kubectl cluster-info to confirm connectivity to the remote Cluster. The output will be the same as in the previous section.

Summary

In this chapter, we've guided you on creating a Kubernetes Cluster. Now that you're ready, the next chapter will finally be a first hands-on Arc experience: deploying your first Data Controller.

CHAPTER 5

Deploying a Data Controller in Indirect Mode

In the previous chapter, we've deployed a Kubernetes Cluster. Now it's time to use this Cluster and deploy our first Azure Arc-enabled Data Controller to it, which we will deploy using indirectly connected – or in short, indirect – mode.

Note   If you are using multiple Kubernetes Clusters, make sure your current context – which is basically the active Kubernetes Cluster configuration – is looking at the right one.

Deciding on a Kubernetes Storage Class

First, double-check that your current context is the one you're targeting with your deployment using Listing 5-1.

Listing 5-1. Retrieve active Kubernetes context

```
kubectl config current-context
```

Our example output in Figure 5-1 shows that we currently have our kubeadm Cluster, which we've previously deployed, as the active context.

© Ben Weissman and Anthony E. Nocentino 2022
B. Weissman and A. E. Nocentino, *Azure Arc-enabled Data Services Revealed*,
https://doi.org/10.1007/978-1-4842-8085-0_5

```
C:\>kubectl config current-context
kubeadm
```

Figure 5-1. *Output example*

As we are already connected to the correct Cluster, we will need to figure out which Storage Classes are available within the Cluster, as this information is required later during the deployment, even if there is just one Storage Class. The Storage Classes can be listed using the command in Listing 5-2.

Listing 5-2. Retrieve list of Storage Classes in current Kubernetes context

```
kubectl get storageclass
```

In our example, there is only one class – local-storage – as shown in Figure 5-2.

```
C:\>kubectl get storageclass
NAME                      PROVISIONER                     RECLAIMPOLICY   VOLUMEBINDINGMODE     ALLOWVOLUMEEXPANSION   AGE
local-storage (default)   kubernetes.io/no-provisioner    Delete          WaitForFirstConsumer  false                  114m
```

Figure 5-2. *List of Storage Classes*

Write this information down or memorize it. In case you are working on a Cluster with multiple Storage Classes available, start thinking which Storage Class you want to use for your Cluster. You can use different Storage Classes for Kubernetes logs, data, and database logs.

Deployment Through the Command Line

As we've introduced in Chapter 2, most deployments around Azure Arc-enabled Data Services are controlled through a tool called *az – the azure-cli*. Even graphical installations from Azure Data Studio simply call this CLI in the background, which is why we'll start with the command-line-driven approach.

A deployment command could, for example, look like Listing 5-3.

Listing 5-3. azure-cli command to create a Data Controller

```
az arcdata dc create     --connectivity-mode Indirect `
                         --name arc-dc-local `
```

```
--k8s-namespace arc `
--subscription <Subscription ID> `
-g arcBook `
-l eastus `
--storage-class local-storage `
--profile-name azure-arc-kubeadm `
--infrastructure onpremises `
--use-k8s
```

This would trigger a Data Controller to be deployed in the current Kubernetes context in indirect mode, the name of the Arc Cluster would be "arc-dc-local," and the Namespace in Kubernetes would be "arc." The subscription ID would need to be replaced with your Azure subscription ID. The deployment would be linked to our resource group "arcBook" in the "East US" region (although the deployment won't show up in the portal until you first upload metrics and/or logs – see Chapter 9 for more details), and it would use the "local-storage" Storage Class.

We are providing a deployment profile name, in our case "azure-arc-kubeadm." The azure-cli comes with a hand full of pre-configured profiles to make it easy to deploy to different versions of Kubernetes. The list of currently provided profiles can be retrieved using the command in Listing 5-4.

The last two parameters will define the infrastructure (allowed values: ['aws', 'gcp', 'azure', 'alibaba', 'onpremises', 'other', 'auto']) and make the client use the local Kubernetes tooling (triggered by the --use-k8s switch). The alternative to that would be to use the Azure Resource Manager, which is what we'll do for our direct connected Data Controller in the next chapter.

There are a few more parameters, and not all of the mentioned parameters in this example are mandatory. You will find the full reference at *https://docs.microsoft.com/ en-us/cli/azure/arcdata*.

Listing 5-4. Retrieve list of configuration profiles for Arc Data Controllers

```
az arcdata dc config list
```

This command will return the list of supported options as shown in Figure 5-3. Every option will have a preset but adjustable configuration for the specific environment such as storage, security, and network integrations.

```
C:\>az arcdata dc config list
[
    "azure-arc-ake",
    "azure-arc-aks-default-storage",
    "azure-arc-aks-hci",
    "azure-arc-aks-premium-storage",
    "azure-arc-azure-openshift",
    "azure-arc-eks",
    "azure-arc-gke",
    "azure-arc-kubeadm",
    "azure-arc-openshift"
]
```

Figure 5-3. *List of configuration profiles for Arc Data Controllers*

Should your desired platform not be on the list or you need changes to the profile's default, you can also start by creating a custom configuration using the code from Listing 5-5.

Listing 5-5. azure-cli command to initialize a custom configuration

```
az arcdata dc config init -p customconfig --source azure-arc-kubeadm
```

This will create a file called *control.json* in a directory called "customconfig". The file looks similar to what we find in Listing 5-6 and can be used to control every configurable parameter of your Data Controller deployment.

Listing 5-6. Sample "control.json" file

```
{
    "apiVersion": "arcdata.microsoft.com/v2",
    "kind": "DataController",
    "metadata": {
        "name": "datacontroller"
    },
```

```json
"spec": {
    "infrastructure": "",
    "credentials": {
        "serviceAccount": "sa-arc-controller",
        "dockerRegistry": "arc-private-registry",
        "domainServiceAccount": "domain-service-account-secret"
    },
    "docker": {
        "registry": "mcr.microsoft.com",
        "repository": "arcdata",
        "imageTag": "v1.1.0_2021-11-02",
        "imagePullPolicy": "Always"
    },
    "storage": {
        "data": {
            "className": "",
            "size": "15Gi",
            "accessMode": "ReadWriteOnce"
        },
        "logs": {
            "className": "",
            "size": "10Gi",
            "accessMode": "ReadWriteOnce"
        }
    },
    "security": {
        "allowDumps": true,
        "allowNodeMetricsCollection": true,
        "allowPodMetricsCollection": true
    },
    "services": [
        {
            "name": "controller",
            "serviceType": "NodePort",
            "port": 30080
        }
```

```
    ],
    "settings": {
        "azure": {
            "autoUploadMetrics": "false",
            "autoUploadLogs": "false"
        },
        "controller": {
            "logs.rotation.size": "5000",
            "logs.rotation.days": "7"
        },
        "ElasticSearch": {
            "vm.max_map_count": "-1"
        }
    }
  }
}
```

If you want to deploy using a custom configuration rather than using pre-configured profile, you can pass the --*profile-name* parameter instead of a *profile name* to the azure-cli as shown in Listing 5-7.

Listing 5-7. azure-cli command to create a Data Controller using a custom config

```
az arcdata dc create      --connectivity-mode Indirect `
                          --name arc-dc-local `
                          --k8s-namespace arc `
                          --subscription <Subscription> `
                          --resource-group arcBook `
                          --location eastus `
                          --profile-name PATH `
                          --use-k8s
```

Whichever way you choose, the CLI will first ask you for the username and password to be used (potentially also to accept the license agreement) and then start with the deployment process. The duration of the process will depend on your target machine's performance and Internet connection, and when done, the output should look similar to what we see in Figure 5-4.

```
C:\>az arcdata dc create --connectivity-mode Indirect --name arc-dc-local --k8s-namespace arc --subscription
 -g arcBook -l eastus --storage-class local-storage --profile-name azure-arc-kubeadm --infrastructure onpremises --use-k8s

Using subscription '                              '.

Monitoring administrator username:arcadmin
Monitoring administrator password:
Confirm Monitoring administrator password:

Deploying data controller

NOTE: Data controller creation can take a significant amount of time depending on
configuration, network speed, and the number of nodes in the cluster.

Data controller successfully deployed.
```

Figure 5-4. *Output of a Data Controller deployment*

If you want to avoid being prompted for EULA, usernames, and passwords, you can also provide them in environment variables:

- ACCEPT_EULA: Set this to "Y"

- AZDATA_USERNAME: The username to be used, for example, arcadmin

- AZDATA_PASSWORD: A strong password of your choice

- AZDATA_LOGSUI_USERNAME and AZDATA_LOGSUI_PASSWORD: Username and password for Logs Dashboard

- AZDATA_METRICSUI_USERNAME and AZDATA_METRICSUI_PASSWORD: Username and password for Metrics Dashboard

---

Note   METRICSUI and LOGSUI will fall back to the AZDATA username/password if they aren't provided.

This would make the azure-cli use those values instead of interactively prompting you. When using environment variables, you can provide dedicated users for the Logs UI, the Metrics UI, and the Controller itself. When entering them interactively, they will all use the same credentials.

If you want to monitor the deployment on the Kubernetes end, you can run the *kubectl* command in Listing 5-8 to follow the progress.

Listing 5-8. Monitor deployment status using kubectl

```
kubectl get pods -n arc --watch
```

Using the *--watch* switch, the output will keep updating whenever the status or number of ready containers in a Pod changes. The output will look like Figure 5-5 and will constantly update when a Pod's status changes.

```
C:\Users\arc>kubectl get pods -n arc --watch
NAME                    READY   STATUS              RESTARTS   AGE
bootstrapper-76mnz      1/1     Running             0          49s
control-jcjg6           0/2     ContainerCreating   0          19s
controldb-0             0/2     ContainerCreating   0          19s
```

Figure 5-5. *Output of Listing 5-8*

Once the deployment has finished, you can use **az** to, for example, retrieve the Controller's endpoints using Listing 5-9.

Listing 5-9. azure-cli command to retrieve a list of endpoints

```
az arcdata dc endpoint list -o table -k arc
```

This will show you the endpoints that we can later on use to monitor our Cluster, similar to the output in Figure 5-6.

```
C:\>az arcdata dc endpoint list -o table -k arc
Description          Endpoint                        Name       Protocol
-------------------  ------------------------------  ---------  ----------
Log Search Dashboard https://172.16.1.6:31053/       logsui     https
Metrics Dashboard    https://172.16.1.8:31054/       metricsui  https
```

Figure 5-6. *List of Data Controller endpoints*

Your first Data Controller is now ready, and we'll show you in the upcoming chapters how you can start using it by deploying data instances to it!

Deployment Through Azure Data Studio

If you prefer a GUI-driven approach, you can use Azure Data Studio for that.

Note   If you are using the NodePort service type, you need to ensure that each Data Controller has different port numbers in the control.json file before deployment. You can't have more than one Data Controller on the same Kubernetes Cluster using the same NodePort port numbers as they would have a conflict about the endpoint's Ports!

Let's begin the process of deploying a Data Controller in Azure Data Studio. You can do that by navigating to the AZURE ARC CONTROLLERS section on the connections tab and click "+" as shown in Figure 5-7.

Figure 5-7. *Start Arc Controller Deployment Wizard*

The wizard will first confirm that you want to deploy data as shown in Figure 5-8.

Select the deployment options

Filter resources...

Categories

All

Hybrid

SQL Server

PostgreSQL

Azure Arc data controller (preview)

Creates an Azure Arc data controller

Figure 5-8. Arc Controller Deployment Wizard – select deployment options

It will then verify that all required tools have been installed in the correct version as shown in Figure 5-9.

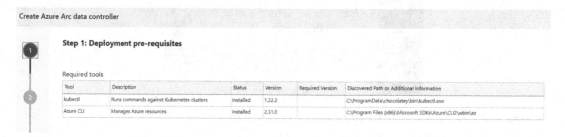

Create Azure Arc data controller

Step 1: Deployment pre-requisites

Required tools

Tool	Description	Status	Version	Required Version	Discovered Path or Additional Information
kubectl	Runs commands against Kubernetes clusters	Installed	1.22.2		C:\ProgramData\chocolatey\bin\kubectl.exe
Azure CLI	Manages Azure resources	Installed	2.31.0		C:\Program Files (x86)\Microsoft SDKs\Azure\CLI2\wbin\az

Figure 5-9. Arc Controller Deployment Wizard – prerequisites

In the next step (Figure 5-10), you will set the Kubernetes context to be used for this deployment.

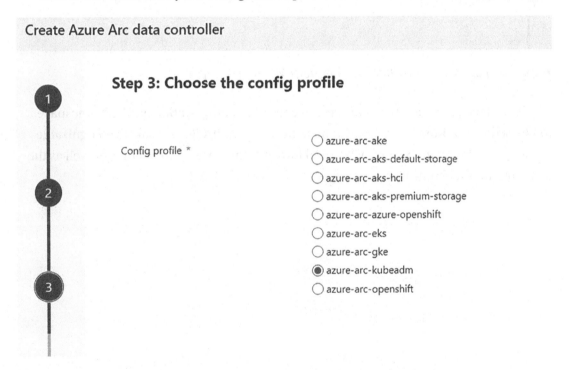

Figure 5-10. *Arc Controller Deployment Wizard – step 2*

This will be followed by the configuration profile to be used as shown in Figure 5-11.

Figure 5-11. *Arc Controller Deployment Wizard – step 3*

The fourth step, which is shown in Figure 5-12, will ask for the Azure configuration to be used for deployment. This consists of your Azure account, subscription, and resource group as well as the location to be used.

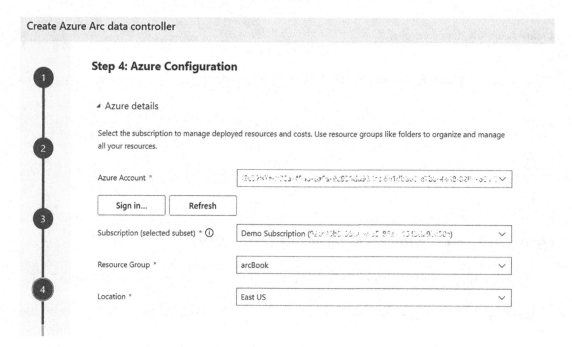

Figure 5-12. *Arc Controller Deployment Wizard – step 4*

Step 5 (see Figure 5-13) will define the controller configuration, so the Namespace to be used within Kubernetes, the name of the Data Controller to make it recognizable in the Azure Portal, the Storage Class and infrastructure type, a username, as well as the password for this Controller.

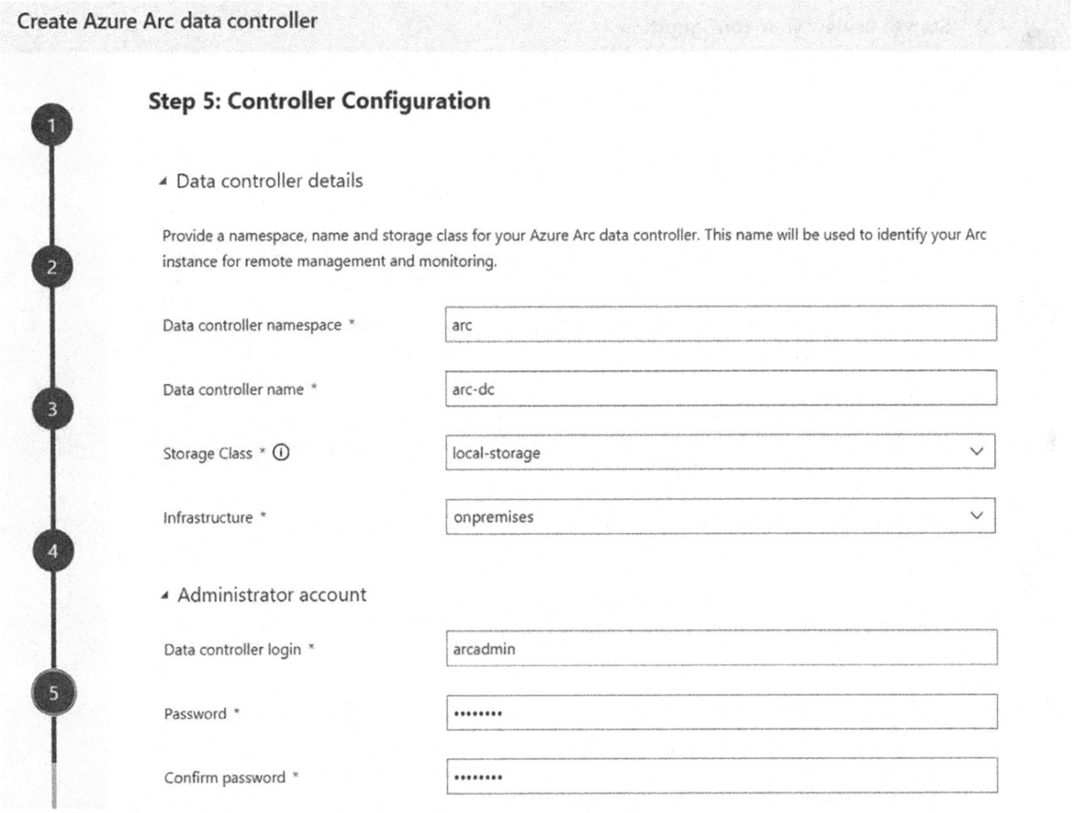

Figure 5-13. *Arc Controller Deployment Wizard – step 5*

The final step 6 will simply provide you a summary of your chosen settings as shown in Figure 5-14.

Figure 5-14. *Arc Controller Deployment Wizard – step 6*

You can confirm these settings using the "Script to notebook" button at the bottom which will create a python-based Jupyter Notebook which can be executed using the "Run all" button (see Figure 5-15) or deploy right away using the "Deploy" button.

Figure 5-15. *Run all button for a Jupyter Notebook in Azure Data Studio*

Since we already deployed a Data Controller, we can skip this part.

In Azure Data Studio, we can also add our existing Controller so it can be managed from here. To do so, click the "Connect Controller" button as shown in Figure 5-16.

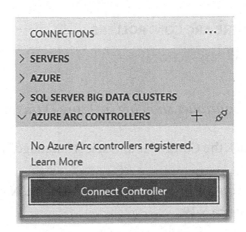

Figure 5-16. *Add Arc Controller to Azure Data Studio*

This will trigger a dialog that requires your Controller's Namespace and Cluster (see Figure 5-17).

Connect to Existing Controller

Namespace *

| arc |

Kube Config File Path *

| C:\Users\PSDemo\.kube\config | Browse |

Cluster Context *

◉ kubeadm

Name ⑦

| |

Figure 5-17. *Add Arc Controller to Azure Data Studio – connection details*

Once you've provided these settings and added the Controller, it will show up in ADS (see Figure 5-18).

Figure 5-18. *Arc Data Controller showing in Azure Data Studio*

If you right-mouse-click the Controller and select "manage," the Controller's settings will be shown.

On the settings page, you will once again see its endpoint, Namespace, etc. An example can be seen in Figure 5-19.

Figure 5-19. *Arc Data Controller Management page in Azure Data Studio*

You have now deployed an Arc Data Controller and added it to the inventory that can be managed from Azure Data Studio.

Summary and Key Takeaways

In this chapter, we've deployed our first Azure Arc Data Controller – in indirect mode.

The next chapter, on the other hand, will walk you through the setup of a directly connected Cluster.

CHAPTER 6

Deploying a Data Controller in Direct Mode

While we've started deploying our first Data Controller in the previous chapter, where we've used the indirectly connected mode, let's also take a look at direct mode Data Controllers. Unlike an indirectly connected Controller, a direct mode Controller will constantly be connected to the Azure Portal, meaning that you don't have to manually upload any usage or log data and also can use this Controller's data for real-time analysis and alerting.

Note   Depending on the type of Kubernetes Cluster you are using, you may not be able to deploy this direct mode Data Controller to the same Cluster due to conflicting ports and resources.

If you are using a kubeadm-based Cluster as described in this book, delete the indirectly connected Data Controller first, or deploy a second Kubernetes Cluster. While it is possible to run a direct and indirect Data Controller on the same Cluster in parallel, this requires a few extra steps, and the use cases for this are so slim that it's out of scope for this book.

Get Your Kubernetes Cluster Azure Arc-enabled

The first requirement for a Data Controller to be deployable in direct mode is for your Kubernetes Cluster to be Azure Arc-enabled. As explained in Chapter 2, Azure Arc has a multitude of offerings, one of them being Azure Arc-enabled Kubernetes.

© Ben Weissman and Anthony E. Nocentino 2022
B. Weissman and A. E. Nocentino, *Azure Arc-enabled Data Services Revealed*,
https://doi.org/10.1007/978-1-4842-8085-0_6

To make the Cluster from your current kubectl Cluster context Arc-enabled, you can use the command shown in Listing 6-1, providing the name for the Cluster in Azure as well as the resource group and location where its metadata should be stored.

Listing 6-1. azure-cli command to make a Kubernetes Cluster Arc-enabled

```
az connectedk8s connect --name kubeadm --resource-group arcBook
--location eastus
```

This results in an output similar to the one in Figure 6-1.

```
C:\>az connectedk8s connect --name kubeadm --resource-group arcBook --location eastus -o table
This operation might take a while...
```

Figure 6-1. *Output of Listing 6-1*

You can also list all Arc-enabled Kubernetes Clusters in a resource group using the command in Listing 6-2.

Listing 6-2. azure-cli command to list the Arc-enabled Kubernetes Clusters in a resource group

```
az connectedk8s list --resource-group arcBook --output table
```

As you can see in Figure 6-2, our kubeadm Cluster has been onboarded and is showing in the output of our command.

```
C:\>az connectedk8s list --resource-group arcBook --output table
Name        Location     ResourceGroup
-------     ----------   ----------------
kubeadm     eastus       arcBook
```

Figure 6-2. *Output of Listing 6-2*

The onboarding or Arc enablement created a Namespace called Azure Arc in our Cluster including a variety of Deployments and Pods which we can list and verify using the command in Listing 6-3.

Listing 6-3. kubectl command to list the Deployments and Pods in the Arc-enabled Namespace

```
kubectl get deployments,pods -n azure-arc
```

Figure 6-3 is showing the result of that command.

```
C:\>kubectl get deployments,pods -n azure-arc
NAME                                        READY   UP-TO-DATE   AVAILABLE   AGE
deployment.apps/cluster-metadata-operator   1/1     1            1           9m55s
deployment.apps/clusterconnect-agent        1/1     1            1           9m55s
deployment.apps/clusteridentityoperator     1/1     1            1           9m55s
deployment.apps/config-agent                1/1     1            1           9m55s
deployment.apps/controller-manager          1/1     1            1           9m55s
deployment.apps/extension-manager           1/1     1            1           9m55s
deployment.apps/flux-logs-agent             1/1     1            1           9m55s
deployment.apps/kube-aad-proxy              1/1     1            1           9m55s
deployment.apps/metrics-agent               1/1     1            1           9m55s
deployment.apps/resource-sync-agent         1/1     1            1           9m55s

NAME                                           READY   STATUS    RESTARTS   AGE
pod/cluster-metadata-operator-9568b899c-hpct6   2/2    Running   0          9m55s
pod/clusterconnect-agent-576758886d-x4wbn       3/3    Running   0          9m55s
pod/clusteridentityoperator-7657dd57f5-sk9d8    2/2    Running   0          9m55s
pod/config-agent-5847569d46-vjtzg               2/2    Running   0          9m55s
pod/controller-manager-df6d56db5-hk26l          2/2    Running   0          9m55s
pod/extension-manager-6f8f595789-ktcf6          2/2    Running   0          9m55s
pod/flux-logs-agent-6db9687fcb-77929            1/1    Running   0          9m55s
pod/kube-aad-proxy-68f4ff6bd4-5jn42             2/2    Running   0          9m55s
pod/metrics-agent-575c565fd9-f88f5              2/2    Running   0          9m55s
pod/resource-sync-agent-6bbd8bcd86-x7nzt        2/2    Running   0          9m55s
```

Figure 6-3. *Output of Listing 6-3*

Once we have successfully connected the Cluster, we also need to enable the custom-locations feature using the command from Listing 6-4. This command doesn't create a custom location yet – it only enables the Cluster to allow the creation of them. A custom location is basically a pointer to our Kubernetes Cluster from Azure so we can address this Cluster when deploying our Data Controller, and while we could create this location from the command line as well, we'll simply do that as part of the Data Controller's deployment process from the Azure Portal later.

Listing 6-4. azure-cli command to enable the custom-locations feature

```
az connectedk8s enable-features -n kubeadm -g arcBook --features cluster-
connect custom-locations
```

Once the feature has been successfully enabled, the CLI will report back as shown in Figure 6-4.

```
C:\>az connectedk8s enable-features -n kubeadm -g arcBook --features cluster-connect custom-locations
This command is in preview and under development. Reference and support levels: https://aka.ms/CLI_refstatus
This operation might take a while...

"Successsfully enabled features: ['cluster-connect', 'custom-locations'] for the Connected Cluster kubeadm"
```

Figure 6-4. *Output of Listing 6-4*

The last requirement on our Cluster itself is the Arc-enabled Data Services extension which will bring in the Custom Resource Definitions into your Kubernetes Cluster and the bootstrapper, which can be created using the command in Listing 6-5. This step has to happen once on every Kubernetes Cluster that you want to use directly connected Arc-enabled Data Services on.

Listing 6-5. azure-cli command to install the Arc-enabled Data Services Kubernetes extension

```
az k8s-extension create --name arc-data-location `
--extension-type microsoft.arcdataservices `
--cluster-type connectedClusters `
--cluster-name kubeadm `
--resource-group arcBook `
--scope cluster `
--release-namespace arc-direct `
--config Microsoft.CustomLocation.ServiceAccount=sa-bootstrapper `
--auto-upgrade false
```

It is important that this step succeeds, so double-check its status using the command in Listing 6-6.

Listing 6-6. azure-cli command to show the status of an Arc-enabled Data Services Kubernetes extension

```
az k8s-extension show --name arc-data-location --cluster-type
connectedClusters -c kubeadm -g arcBook -o table
```

As you can see in Figure 6-5, the ProvisioningState is showing as Succeeded – do not proceed until this is the case, which can take a few minutes.

```
C:\>az k8s-extension show --name arc-data-location --cluster-type connectedClusters -c kubeadm -g arcBook -o table

Name                ExtensionType              Version         ProvisioningState   LastModifiedAt
-----------------   ------------------------   ------------    -----------------   ----------------------------------
arc-data-location   microsoft.arcdataservices  1.1.17561007    Succeeded           2021-12-09T15:20:58.075329+00:00
```

Figure 6-5. *Output of Listing 6-6*

As mentioned, this also created a bootstrapper in our Cluster which we can list using the kubectl command in Listing 6-7.

Listing 6-7. kubectl command to list all Pods in a Namespace

```
kubectl get pods -n arc-direct
```

The output, which should look similar to the one in Figure 6-6, confirms that our bootstrapper Pod has been created and is running.

```
C:\>kubectl get pods -n arc-direct
NAME                          READY   STATUS    RESTARTS   AGE
bootstrapper-66c7779f5f-6tcmd 1/1     Running   0          95s
```

Figure 6-6. *Output of Listing 6-7*

Our Kubernetes Cluster is now ready for the deployment of a directly connected Azure Arc Data Controller.

Get Your Azure Subscription Ready

In addition to the requirements to your Kubernetes Cluster, there is also a requirement in your Azure subscription: we need a Log Analytics Workspace. Should you already have one, feel free to use that. Otherwise, you can create one using the command in Listing 6-8. The important part is that the Workspace needs a unique name.

Listing 6-8. azure-cli command to create a Log Analytics Workspace

```
az monitor log-analytics workspace create -g arcBook -n arcBookLAWS
```

The result, which should look similar to the one in Figure 6-7, is in JSON format.

```
C:\>az monitor log-analytics workspace create -g arcBook -n arcBookLAWS
{
  "createdDate": "Thu, 09 Dec 2021 15:37:56 GMT",
  "customerId": "                              ",
  "eTag": null,
  "features": {
    "clusterResourceId": null,
    "disableLocalAuth": null,
    "enableDataExport": null,
    "enableLogAccessUsingOnlyResourcePermissions": true,
    "immediatePurgeDataOn30Days": null,
    "legacy": 0,
    "searchVersion": 1
  },
  "forceCmkForQuery": null,
  "id": "/subscriptions/92cc49b9-95ca-4935-86e1-1545d29bc50a/resourcegroups/arcbook/providers/microsoft.operational
insights/workspaces/arcbooklaws",
```

Figure 6-7. *Output of Listing 6-8*

To access this workspace, we need its primary access key, which can be retrieved through the command in Listing 6-9.

Listing 6-9. azure-cli command to retrieve a workspace's shared keys

```
az monitor log-analytics workspace get-shared-keys -g arcBook -n
arcBookLAWS
```

The output will again be in JSON format as the one in Figure 6-8. Copy the value of the *primarySharedKey*, as we'll need it when setting up our Data Controller.

```
C:\>az monitor log-analytics workspace get-shared-keys -g arcBook -n arcBookLAWS
{
  "primarySharedKey": "Pe8QfyVlKv7YfV5INiuuotZW/9UQpanpnSI37T9rAh9kAa8JrODYVQFMEFtIegEnBKdP/JGFOjhtS3LJXGe7dW==",
  "secondarySharedKey": "LFLiVHvskrzk1Y4Xoefjv20O5Q06+ktuEWTk9IjfFPO3rUxBNdzIv+nbfZ+kF8cJIMI5Wtf5C4535iKjgxIFlA=="
}
```

Figure 6-8. *Access key for Azure Log Analytics Workspace*

Our Log Analytics Workspace is now also ready to be used with our Data Controller.

Deploy a Direct Mode Data Controller

Since a directly connected Azure Arc Data Controller is basically an Azure resource like any other (despite only its metadata residing in Azure), we could also deploy it through the CLI or an ARM template, for example.

We'll however focus on the approach through the Azure Portal. Feel free to reuse the resulting ARM template from this process – we just think that it is super cool how you can deploy a resource online in the Portal which will then show up in our on-premises Kubernetes Cluster.

To start the deployment, navigate to the Create Azure Arc Data Controller blade in the Portal at *https://portal.azure.com/#create/Microsoft.DataController*, and select that you're planning to use an Azure Arc-enabled Kubernetes Cluster, so direct connectivity mode, as shown in Figure 6-9.

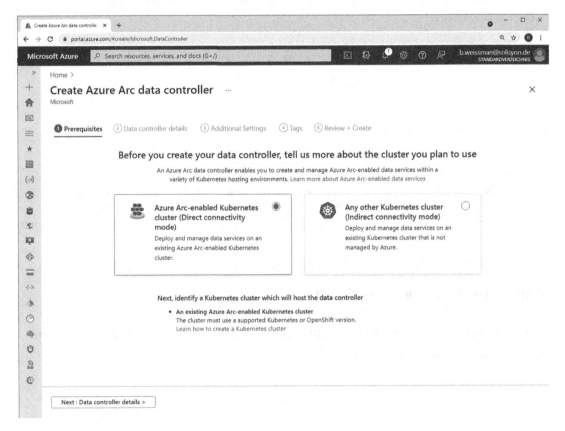

Figure 6-9. *Create Azure Arc Data Controller in Azure Portal*

On the next screen, as visible in Figure 6-10, you'll start by providing a subscription and resource group to be used for your Data Controller's metadata as well as a name for the Controller.

Home >

Create Azure Arc data controller ⋯
Microsoft

✅ Prerequisites   ② **Data controller details**   ③ Additional Settings   ④ Tags   ⑤ Review + Create

Create an Azure Arc data controller to enable Azure data services in the Kubernetes environment of your choice.

Project details

Select the subscription to manage deployed resources and costs. Use resource groups like folders to organize and manage all your resources.

Subscription * ⓘ	Demo Subscription ⌄
Resource group * ⓘ	arcBook ⌄

Data controller details

Provide a name to identify your data controller for remote management and monitoring.

> ⓘ This data controller will be installed in direct connectivity mode to an existing Azure Arc-enabled Kubernetes cluster. This connectivity mode will allow you to create and manage Arc-enabled data services, such as Arc-enabled SQL Managed Instance and Arc-enabled PostgreSQL Hyperscale, directly from the Azure portal.

Data controller name *	arc-dc-direct ✓

***Figure 6-10.** Data Controller details*

On the same screen, you will need to either select the custom location to be used or create one as shown in Figure 6-11.

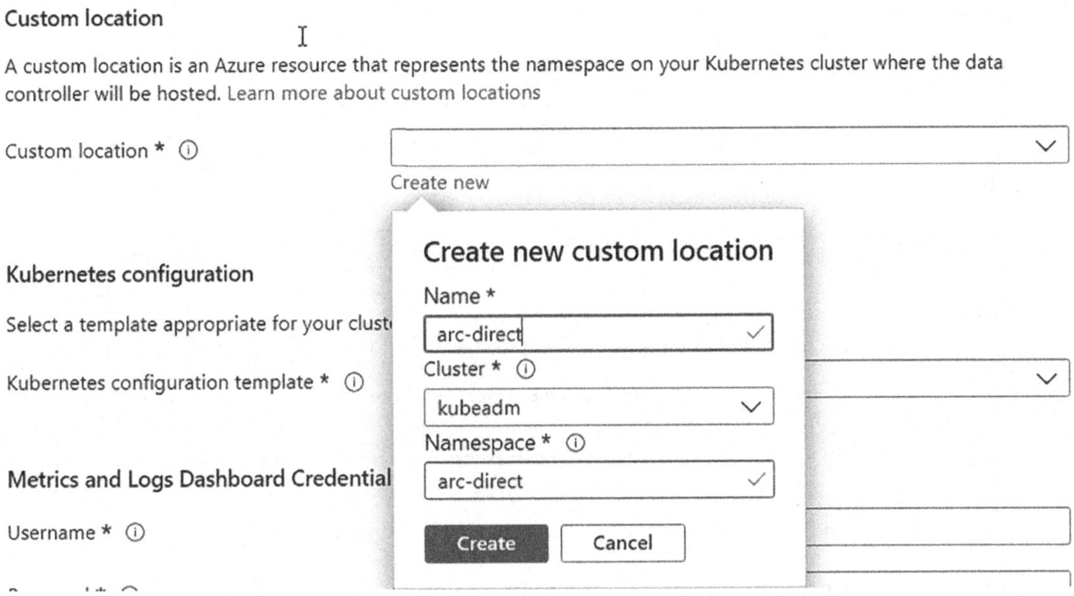

Custom location

A custom location is an Azure resource that represents the namespace on your Kubernetes cluster where the data controller will be hosted. Learn more about custom locations

Custom location * ⓘ

Create new

Create new custom location

Name *

arc-direct

Cluster * ⓘ

kubeadm

Namespace * ⓘ

arc-direct

Create   Cancel

Kubernetes configuration

Select a template appropriate for your clust

Kubernetes configuration template * ⓘ

Metrics and Logs Dashboard Credential

Username * ⓘ

Figure 6-11. *Create new custom location*

Still on the same, first screen, we will also provide the Kubernetes configuration – information like Storage Classes, etc., which we've provided through the command line in the previous chapter as well as the service type and the credentials to be used for the built-in dashboards for metrics and logs (Figure 6-12).

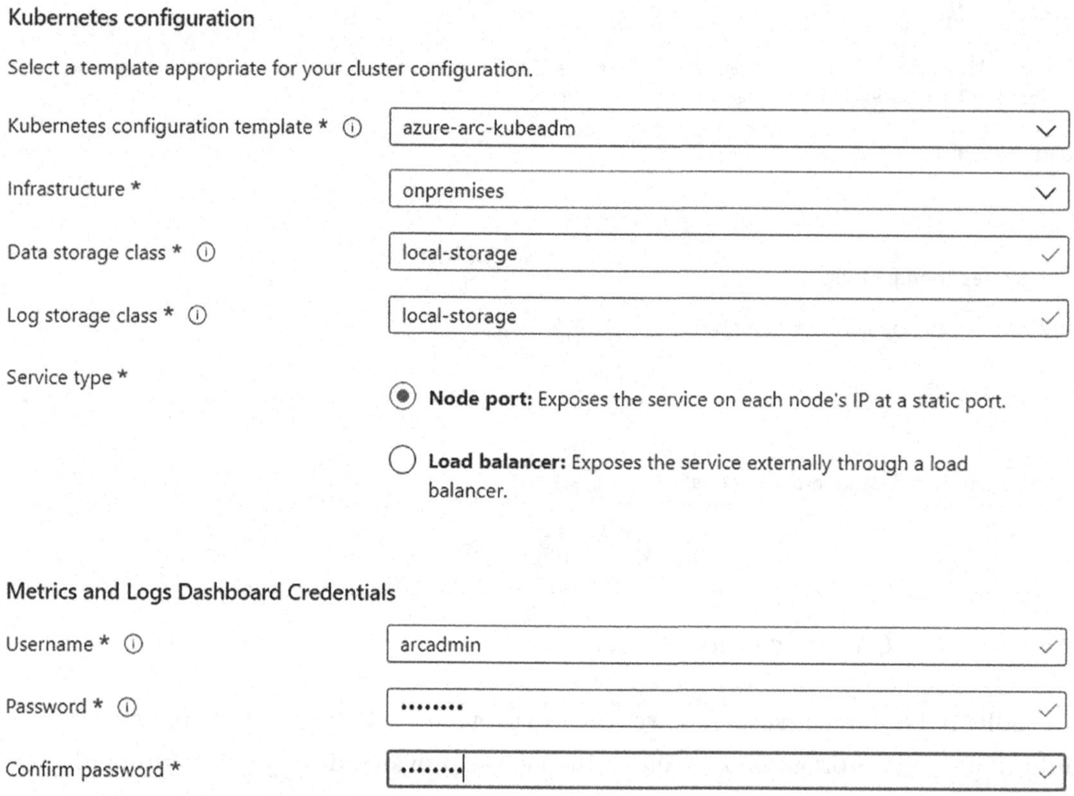

Kubernetes configuration

Select a template appropriate for your cluster configuration.

Kubernetes configuration template * ⓘ	azure-arc-kubeadm ⌄
Infrastructure *	onpremises ⌄
Data storage class * ⓘ	local-storage ✓
Log storage class * ⓘ	local-storage ✓

Service type *

    ⦿ **Node port:** Exposes the service on each node's IP at a static port.

    ○ **Load balancer:** Exposes the service externally through a load balancer.

Metrics and Logs Dashboard Credentials

Username * ⓘ	arcadmin ✓
Password * ⓘ	•••••••• ✓
Confirm password *	•••••••• ✓

Figure 6-12. *Kubernetes configuration and dashboard credentials*

Moving on to the next screen "Additional Settings" (see Figure 6-13), we can enable or disable the automatic uploads of metrics and logs. It is highly recommended to keep them both enabled to make sure you benefit from features like real-time alerts. When activating them, you will also need to select the Log Analytics Workspace to be used and provide its primary key which we've retrieved earlier through Listing 6-9.

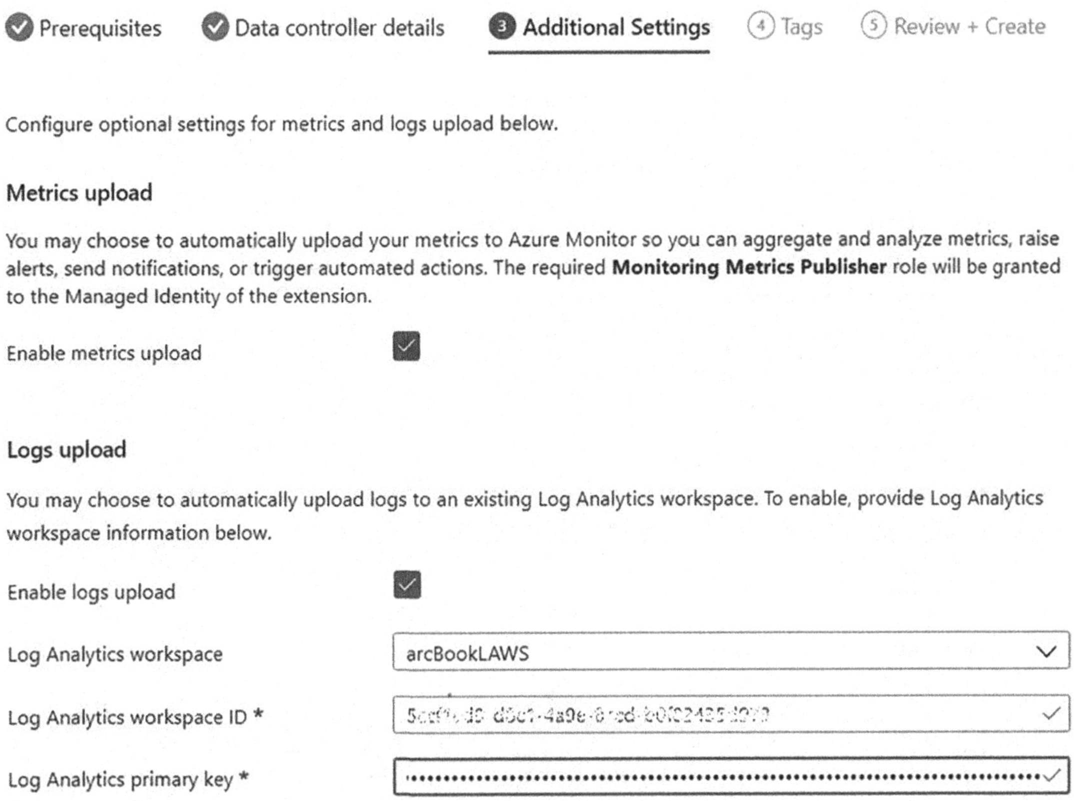

✅ Prerequisites   ✅ Data controller details   ③ **Additional Settings**   ④ Tags   ⑤ Review + Create

Configure optional settings for metrics and logs upload below.

Metrics upload

You may choose to automatically upload your metrics to Azure Monitor so you can aggregate and analyze metrics, raise alerts, send notifications, or trigger automated actions. The required **Monitoring Metrics Publisher** role will be granted to the Managed Identity of the extension.

Enable metrics upload   ☑

Logs upload

You may choose to automatically upload logs to an existing Log Analytics workspace. To enable, provide Log Analytics workspace information below.

Enable logs upload   ☑

Log Analytics workspace | arcBookLAWS   ∨ |

Log Analytics workspace ID * | 5ccf9cd9-d0c1-4a9e-8ncd-b0f02435f0f0   ✓ |

Log Analytics primary key * | ••✓ |

Figure 6-13. *Metrics and logs upload*

In the last configuration step, visible in Figure 6-14, you can provide tags for the Data Controller which is especially helpful when using multiple Controllers in different locations.

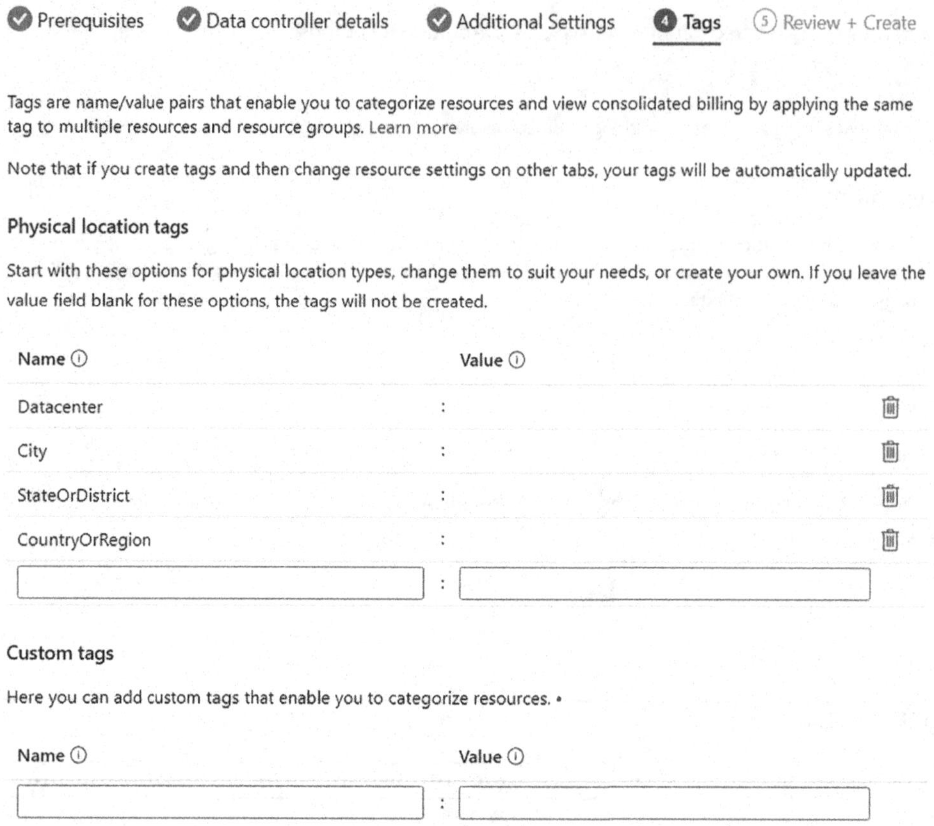

✔ Prerequisites   ✔ Data controller details   ✔ Additional Settings   ④ Tags   ⑤ Review + Create

Tags are name/value pairs that enable you to categorize resources and view consolidated billing by applying the same tag to multiple resources and resource groups. Learn more

Note that if you create tags and then change resource settings on other tabs, your tags will be automatically updated.

Physical location tags

Start with these options for physical location types, change them to suit your needs, or create your own. If you leave the value field blank for these options, the tags will not be created.

Name ⓘ		Value ⓘ	
Datacenter	:		🗑
City	:		🗑
StateOrDistrict	:		🗑
CountryOrRegion	:		🗑
	:		

Custom tags

Here you can add custom tags that enable you to categorize resources. •

Name ⓘ		Value ⓘ
	:	

Figure 6-14. *Azure tags*

From there, you can finalize the deployment and create the Data Controller which will confirm back similarly as shown in Figure 6-15.

✅ Your deployment is complete

Deployment name: arc-dc-direct   Start time: 12/9/2021, 3:44:44 PM
Subscription: Demo Subscription   Correlation ID: bf2d50c3-e81a-416f-9112-4e09d628d560
Resource group: arcBook

∧ **Deployment details** (Download)

	Resource	Type	Status	Operation details
✅	arc-dc-direct	Microsoft.AzureArcData/dat...	OK	Operation details
✅	arc-direct	Microsoft.ExtendedLocation...	OK	Operation details
✅	1cb4e41a-9b52-4b13-b53a-ef	Microsoft.Authorization/rol...	Created	Operation details
✅	08d9ea87-51b2-4df8-a4b5-d8	Microsoft.Authorization/rol...	Created	Operation details

∧ **Next steps**

   Go to resource group

Figure 6-15. *Deployment complete*

Our new Azure Arc Data Controller will also show up in our resource group immediately as you can see in Figure 6-16.

Subscription (Move)   Deployments
Demo Subscription   1 Succeeded

Subscription ID   Location
.. ..   East US

Tags (Edit)
Click here to add tags

Resources   Recommendations

[Filter for any field...]   (Type == **all** ✕)   (Location == **all** ✕)   ⁺▽ Add filter

Showing 1 to 4 of 4 records.   ☐ Show hidden types ⓘ   [No grouping   ∨]   [List view   ∨]

☐ Name ↑↓	Type ↑↓	Location ↑↓	
☐ 🗄 arc-dc-direct	Azure Arc data controller	East US	•••
☐ 🧩 arc-direct	Custom location	East US	•••
☐ 🗂 arcBookLAWS	Log Analytics workspace	East US	•••
☐ ⛓ kubeadm	Kubernetes - Azure Arc	East US	•••

Figure 6-16. *Data Controller showing in Azure Resource Group*

This only means, however, that the deployment command has been sent to the Kubernetes Cluster. We can monitor the actual deployment through kubectl using the command in Listing 6-10.

Listing 6-10. kubectl command to list Pods in Namespace

```
kubectl get pods -n arc-direct
```

As you can see in Figure 6-17, the first few Pods have been started to create alongside our pre-existing bootstrapper.

```
C:\>kubectl get pods -n arc-direct
NAME                               READY   STATUS            RESTARTS   AGE
bootstrapper-66c7779f5f-6tcmd      1/1     Running           0          24m
control-bvqv8                      0/2     Pending           0          8s
controldb-0                        0/2     ContainerCreating 0          8s
```

Figure 6-17. *Pods in Arc-direct Namespace during deployment*

If you rerun the command from Listing 6-10 after a while, you should see all the Pods of a Data Controller, similar to the ones from our indirect mode deployment in the previous chapter, shown in Figure 6-18.

```
C:\>kubectl get pods -n arc-direct
NAME                               READY   STATUS    RESTARTS   AGE
bootstrapper-66c7779f5f-6tcmd      1/1     Running   0          28m
control-bvqv8                      2/2     Running   0          4m29s
controldb-0                        2/2     Running   0          4m29s
logsdb-0                           3/3     Running   0          3m39s
logsui-8b272                       3/3     Running   0          107s
metricsdb-0                        2/2     Running   0          3m39s
metricsdc-cg9zv                    2/2     Running   0          3m39s
metricsdc-dn2sx                    2/2     Running   0          3m39s
metricsdc-vsk5q                    2/2     Running   0          3m39s
metricsui-16w6z                    2/2     Running   0          3m39s
```

Figure 6-18. *Pods in Arc-direct Namespace after deployment*

You can also verify the status of this Data Controller using the command from Listing 6-11.

Listing 6-11. azure-cli command to retrieve a Data Controller's status

```
az arcdata dc status show --k8s-namespace arc-direct --use-k8s
```

As shown in Figure 6-19, the Controller is showing as ready.

```
C:\>az arcdata dc status show --k8s-namespace arc-direct --use-k8s
Ready
```

Figure 6-19. *Data Controller status*

To add this Cluster in Azure Data Studio, simply use the same process as when adding the indirect mode Controller and provide the Controller's Kubernetes Namespace as shown in Figure 6-20.

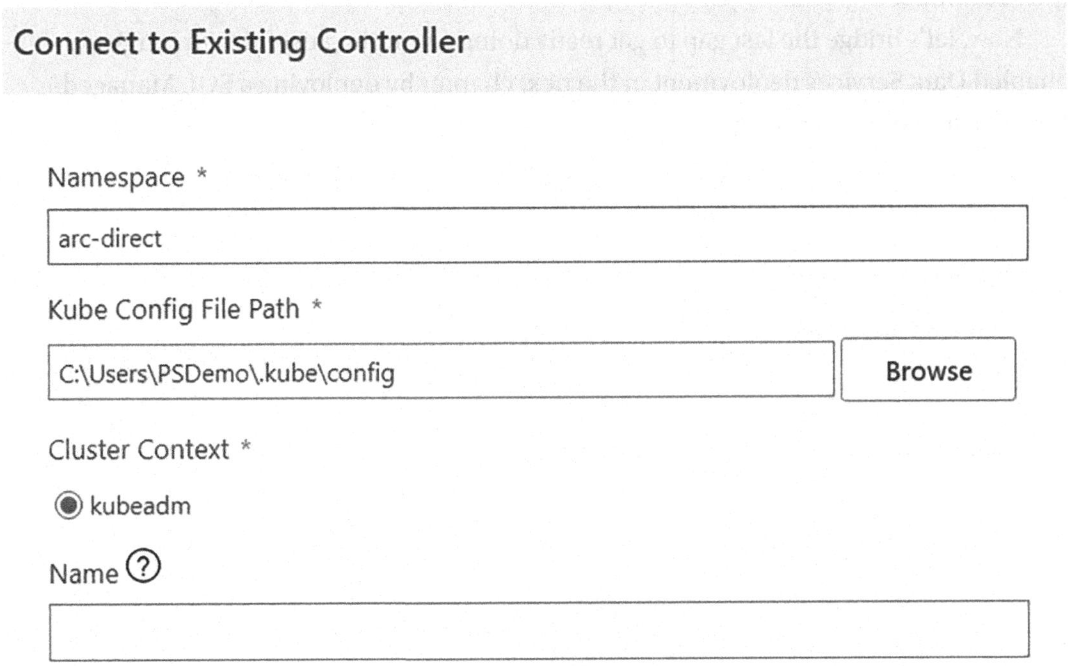

Figure 6-20. *Connect existing Data Controller in ADS*

In Azure Data Studio, after adding the Controller, we can also verify again that this Controller is in direct connection mode (Figure 6-21).

Name : arc-dc-direct
Region : East US
Type : Azure Arc Data Controller
Namespace : arc-direct

Resource Group : arcBook
Subscription ID :
Connection Mode : Direct

Figure 6-21. *Data Controller details in ADS*

Our direct connected Data Controller is now manageable and accessible through the Azure Portal, the command line, and Azure Data Studio.

Summary and Key Takeaways

This and the previous chapter got us another big step closer to working with our first instance of Arc-enabled Data Services by deploying Data Controllers in either direct or indirect mode.

Now, let's bridge the last gap to get ready doing something useful with our Arc-enabled Data Services deployment in the next chapter by deploying a SQL Managed Instance into our Controller.

CHAPTER 7

Deploying an Azure Arc-enabled SQL Managed Instance

With our Data Controllers ready and waiting, we can now go ahead and start deploying a first database instance so we can start working with our Arc-enabled Data Services installation.

Similar to the deployment of the Data Controller, we can either use the command line or a wizard in Azure Data Studio or the Azure Portal for this.

Note All our instance deployments will target an indirectly connected Data Controller unless it's stated otherwise.

Deployment Through the azure-cli

A new Azure Arc-enabled SQL Managed Instance can be deployed through a simple azure-cli command like the one in Listing 7-1. The only required parameters are the name of the instance and the Kubernetes Namespace. The Namespace will be created for you; if it already exists, it must be empty.

Listing 7-1. azure-cli command to create a new Azure Arc SQL MI

```
az sql mi-arc create -n mi-1 --k8s-namespace arc --use-k8s
```

121

© Ben Weissman and Anthony E. Nocentino 2022
B. Weissman and A. E. Nocentino, *Azure Arc-enabled Data Services Revealed*,
https://doi.org/10.1007/978-1-4842-8085-0_7

If you look at the command in Listing 7-2 which would create a regular Managed Instance, you can tell how Azure-native the Arc commands really are.

Listing 7-2. azure-cli command to create a new Azure SQL MI

```
az sql mi create -n mi-1 …
```

The azure-cli will again prompt you for a password unless you provided it through the AZDATA_PASSWORD environment variable and then proceed with the deployment as shown in Figure 7-1.

```
C:\>az sql mi-arc create -n mi-1 --k8s-namespace arc --use-k8s
Arc SQL managed instance username:arcadmin
Arc SQL managed instance password:
Confirm Arc SQL managed instance password:
Deploying mi-1 in namespace `arc`
mi-1 is Ready
```

Figure 7-1. *Output of SQL MI deployment command*

Once the deployment – which should only take a few minutes – has completed, we can run a quick az command to list all our instances, which is just this one for now, as shown in Listing 7-3.

Listing 7-3. azure-cli command to list all SQL MIs in the current Controller

```
az sql mi-arc list --k8s-namespace arc --use-k8s -o table
```

The output (similar to Figure 7-2) will include the instance's endpoint, name, state, and its number of replicas.

```
C:\>az sql mi-arc list --k8s-namespace arc --use-k8s -o table
Name      PrimaryEndpoint      Replicas      State
------    ------------------   ----------    -------
mi-1      172.16.1.6,32057     1/1           Ready
```

Figure 7-2. *List of SQL Managed Instances in the current Controller*

If we refresh our Data Controller's management page in Azure Data Studio as shown in Figure 7-3, the instance will also show up.

Figure 7-3. *Arc Data Controller management page in ADS*

When clicking on the instance, we will be led to the instance's dashboard which will once again show its endpoint, status, etc., as displayed in Figure 7-4. The external endpoint shown would also be the endpoint you'd use to connect to this instance using any application including Azure Data Studio or SQL Server Management Studio. Since this is a kubeadm-based Kubernetes Cluster, it will be a NodePort Service. This may differ on other Kubernetes types. On Azure Kubernetes Services, for example, the default would be a LoadBalancer Service.

Figure 7-4. *SQL MI management page in ADS*

Instead of using **az** or Azure Data Studio, you could also look at the Pods that have been deployed using kubectl as shown in Listing 7-4.

Listing 7-4. kubectl command to list Pods in Namespace

```
kubectl get pods -n <Namespace>
```

The result would look similar to the one in Figure 7-5.

```
C:\>kubectl get pods -n arc
NAME                    READY    STATUS      RESTARTS    AGE
bootstrapper-9clg6      1/1      Running     0           105m
control-9frhh           2/2      Running     0           105m
controldb-0             2/2      Running     0           105m
logsdb-0                3/3      Running     0           104m
logsui-9wfww            3/3      Running     0           102m
metricsdb-0             2/2      Running     0           104m
metricsdc-2fdkn         2/2      Running     0           104m
metricsdc-nf4t5         2/2      Running     0           104m
metricsdc-qm291         2/2      Running     0           104m
metricsui-n5lmk         2/2      Running     0           104m
mi-1-0                  4/4      Running     0           12m
mi-1-ha-0               2/2      Running     0           12m
```

Figure 7-5. *Pods in arc Namespace*

Of course, the azure-cli also accepts additional parameters when creating a new Azure Arc-enabled SQL Managed Instance, for example, the Storage Classes.

One of the most interesting parameters though is *replicas*. By default, an Arc SQL Managed Instance will deploy using the General-Purpose tier, so with a single replica. By providing the replicas switch, you can increase the number of replicas to two or three which will make your instance use the Business-Critical tier and automatically deploy an Availability Group with the given number of replicas as shown in Listing 7-5.

Listing 7-5. azure-cli command to create a new SQL Managed Instance with parameters

```
az sql mi-arc create -n mi-2 --k8s-namespace arc --use-k8s
--storage-class-logs local-storage --storage-class-data local-storage
--storage-class-datalogs local-storage --replicas 3
```

With regard to picking appropriate Storage Classes, traditional DBA storage/file layout applies here, and we're using local-storage for the example only. As you can see in Figure 7-6, where we ran kubectl get pods, this will create three rather than just one Pod for your instance, each of them representing a replica. In addition, every Azure Arc-enabled SQL Managed Instance also comes with an *<name>-ha-0* Pod which controls high availability.

```
NAME                  READY   STATUS    RESTARTS   AGE
bootstrapper-9clg6    1/1     Running   0          115m
control-9frhh         2/2     Running   0          115m
controldb-0           2/2     Running   0          115m
logsdb-0              3/3     Running   0          114m
logsui-9wfww          3/3     Running   0          112m
metricsdb-0           2/2     Running   0          114m
metricsdc-2fdkn       2/2     Running   0          114m
metricsdc-nf4t5       2/2     Running   0          114m
metricsdc-qm29l       2/2     Running   0          114m
metricsui-n5lmk       2/2     Running   0          114m
mi-1-0                4/4     Running   0          22m
mi-1-ha-0             2/2     Running   0          22m
mi-2-0                4/4     Running   0          7m11s
mi-2-1                4/4     Running   0          7m11s
mi-2-2                4/4     Running   0          7m11s
mi-2-ha-0             2/2     Running   0          7m11s
```

Figure 7-6. Pods in Arc Namespace

Deployment Through Azure Data Studio

Azure Data Studio can also be used to run a full deployment. On a Data Controller's dashboard, we can find a button "New Instance" (see Figure 7-7).

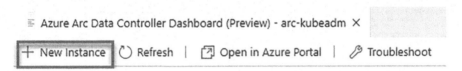

Figure 7-7. New Instance deployment button in Azure Data Studio

This triggers another wizard which will first ask us what kind of an instance we want to create. Pick an Azure SQL Managed Instance as illustrated in Figure 7-8 and accept the terms.

Figure 7-8. *Instance deployment wizard in ADS*

The following screen will ask us to accept the license agreement and check for the prerequisites as shown in Figure 7-9.

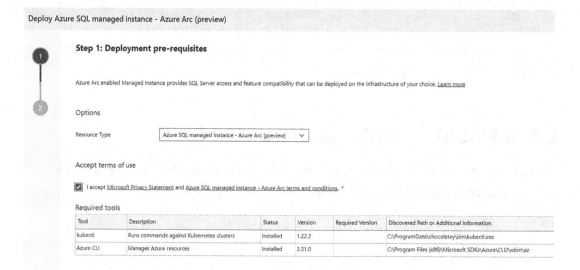

Figure 7-9. *Instance deployment wizard in ADS*

This is followed by the configuration options like Storage Classes for each data type, CPU, and memory requests and limits for this instance (see Figure 7-10). If needed, as introduced in Chapter 2, you could assign different Storage Classes for logs, data, and data logs (transaction logs).

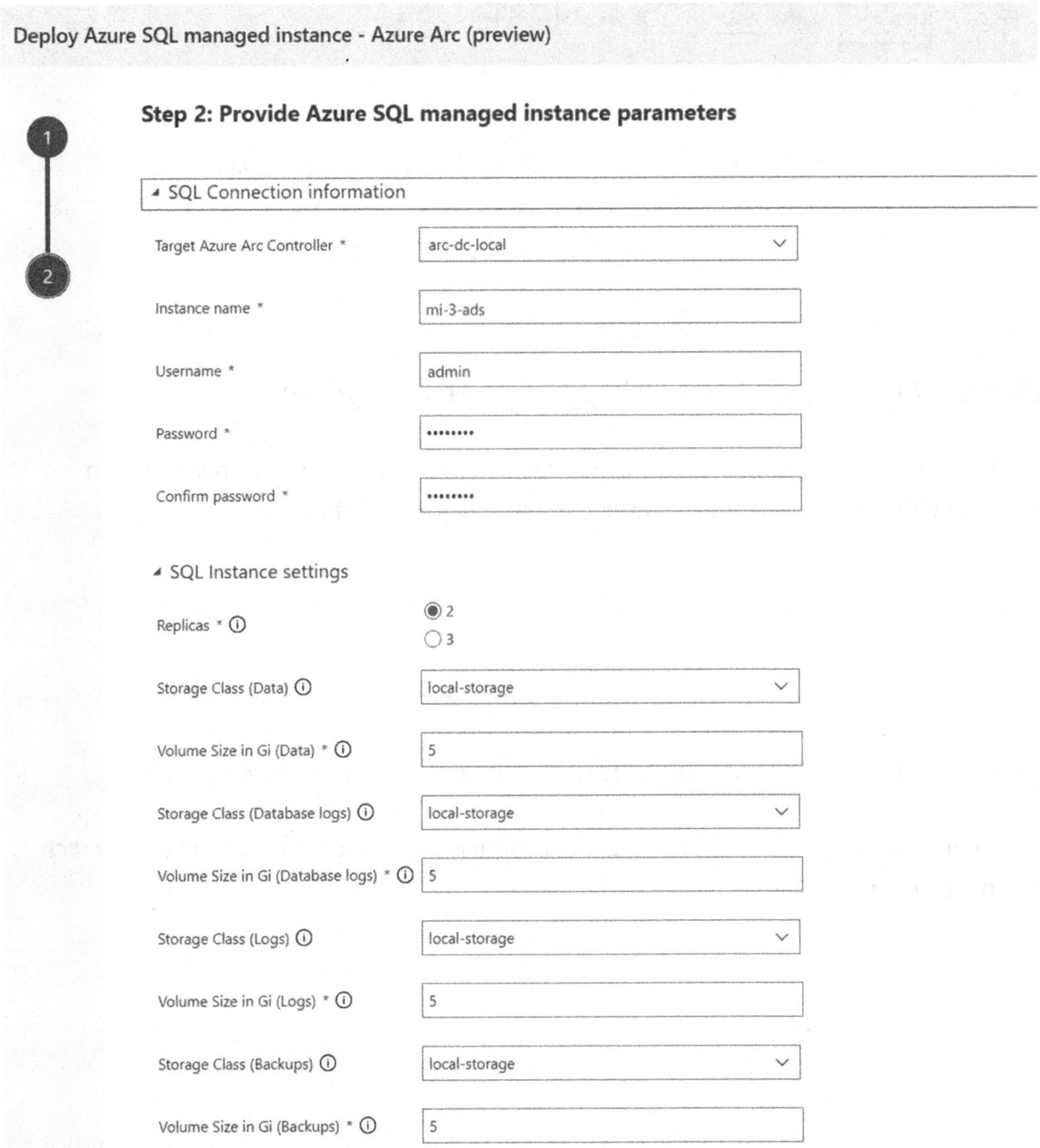

Deploy Azure SQL managed instance - Azure Arc (preview)

Step 2: Provide Azure SQL managed instance parameters

▲ SQL Connection information

Target Azure Arc Controller * | arc-dc-local ⌄ |

Instance name * | mi-3-ads |

Username * | admin |

Password * | •••••••• |

Confirm password * | •••••••• |

▲ SQL Instance settings

Replicas * ⓘ   ◉ 2
                 ○ 3

Storage Class (Data) ⓘ | local-storage ⌄ |

Volume Size in Gi (Data) * ⓘ | 5 |

Storage Class (Database logs) ⓘ | local-storage ⌄ |

Volume Size in Gi (Database logs) * ⓘ | 5 |

Storage Class (Logs) ⓘ | local-storage ⌄ |

Volume Size in Gi (Logs) * ⓘ | 5 |

Storage Class (Backups) ⓘ | local-storage ⌄ |

Volume Size in Gi (Backups) * ⓘ | 5 |

Figure 7-10. Parameters for SQL MI deployment in Azure Data Studio

Completing this page will give you the option to deploy this instance immediately or generate another notebook (just like when we created the Data Controller) which can be run using the "Run all" button as shown in Figure 7-11.

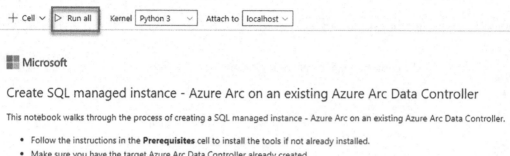

Figure 7-11. *"Run all" button to trigger SQL MI deployment*

While the deployment is running, we can see the instance being created when refreshing the Data Controller's status page (see Figure 7-12).

Azure Arc Resources

Name	Type	State
mi-1	SQL managed instance - Azure Arc	Ready
mi-2	SQL managed instance - Azure Arc	Ready
mi-3-ads	SQL managed instance - Azure Arc	Creating

Figure 7-12. *New SQL MI showing as "Creating" in Azure Data Studio*

Alternatively, we can also monitor the progress using `kubectl get pods --watch` again (see Figure 7-13).

NAME	READY	STATUS	RESTARTS	AGE
bootstrapper-9clg6	1/1	Running	0	121m
control-9frhh	2/2	Running	0	121m
controldb-0	2/2	Running	0	121m
logsdb-0	3/3	Running	0	120m
logsui-9wfww	3/3	Running	0	118m
metricsdb-0	2/2	Running	0	120m
metricsdc-2fdkn	2/2	Running	0	120m
metricsdc-nf4t5	2/2	Running	0	120m
metricsdc-qm29l	2/2	Running	0	120m
metricsui-n5lmk	2/2	Running	0	120m
mi-1-0	4/4	Running	0	28m
mi-1-ha-0	2/2	Running	0	28m
mi-2-0	4/4	Running	0	13m
mi-2-1	4/4	Running	0	13m
mi-2-2	4/4	Running	0	13m
mi-2-ha-0	2/2	Running	0	13m
mi-3-ads-0	3/4	Running	0	41s
mi-3-ads-ha-0	2/2	Running	0	41s

Figure 7-13. *Output of Kubernetes Pod list*

Once the deployment completes, the instance is ready for use.

Deployment Through Kubernetes Tools

As Azure Arc-enabled Data Services aren't only Azure but also Kubernetes native, they can also be deployed through Kubernetes tools, for example, kubectl and a YAML manifest.

Listing 7-6 describes a SQL Managed Instance for us in a YAML manifest.

Listing 7-6. YAML manifest for Arc SQL Managed Instance

```
apiVersion: sql.arcdata.microsoft.com/v2
kind: SqlManagedInstance
metadata:
  name: mi-4
```

```
spec:
  security:
    adminLoginSecret: mi-4-login-secret
  scheduling:
    default:
      resources:
        limits:
          cpu: "2"
          memory: 4Gi
        requests:
          cpu: "1"
          memory: 2Gi
  services:
    primary:
      type: NodePort
  storage:
    backups:
      volumes:
      - className: local-storage
        size: 5Gi
    data:
      volumes:
      - className: local-storage
        size: 5Gi
    datalogs:
      volumes:
      - className: local-storage
        size: 5Gi
    logs:
      volumes:
      - className: local-storage
        size: 5Gi
```

As we also need to authenticate against that Managed Instance, we'll need the username and password for it to be stored in a Kubernetes secret. We can create this Kubernetes secret using the kubectl command in Listing 7-7.

Listing 7-7. kubectl command to create Kubernetes secret

```
kubectl create secret generic mi-4-login-secret `
    --from-literal=password=<pw> `
    --from-literal=username=<user> `
    -n arc
```

Once that has completed, we can use kubectl and our manifest to create our instance (Listing 7-8).

Listing 7-8. kubectl command to create a SQL Managed Instance from YAML

```
kubectl apply -f mi-4.yaml -n arc
```

As you can see in Figure 7-14, this will equally create a Managed Instance for us in our Arc Namespace.

NAME	READY	STATUS	RESTARTS	AGE
bootstrapper-9clg6	1/1	Running	0	133m
control-9frhh	2/2	Running	0	133m
controldb-0	2/2	Running	0	133m
logsdb-0	3/3	Running	0	132m
logsui-9wfww	3/3	Running	0	130m
metricsdb-0	2/2	Running	0	132m
metricsdc-2fdkn	2/2	Running	0	132m
metricsdc-nf4t5	2/2	Running	0	132m
metricsdc-qm29l	2/2	Running	0	132m
metricsui-n5lmk	2/2	Running	0	132m
mi-1-0	4/4	Running	0	40m
mi-1-ha-0	2/2	Running	0	40m
mi-2-0	4/4	Running	0	25m
mi-2-1	4/4	Running	0	25m
mi-2-2	4/4	Running	0	25m
mi-2-ha-0	2/2	Running	0	25m
mi-3-ads-0	4/4	Running	0	12m
mi-3-ads-ha-0	2/2	Running	0	12m
mi-4-0	3/4	Running	0	81s
mi-4-ha-0	2/2	Running	0	81s

Figure 7-14. *Arc Pods in Kubernetes Namespace*

Deployment Through the Azure Portal

Another way of deploying Arc Instances is through the Azure Portal.

Note   Deployment through the Azure Portal requires a directly connected Cluster as showcased in the previous chapter.

Navigate to the "Create a Resource" section in the Portal at *https://portal.azure. com/#create/hub*.

From there, search for "arc sql managed instance" as shown in Figure 7-15.

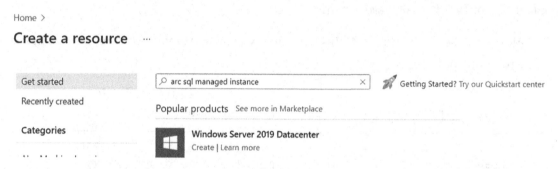

Figure 7-15. Azure Portal – Create a resource

Select the only result showing up (Figure 7-16).

Showing 1 to 1 of 1 results.

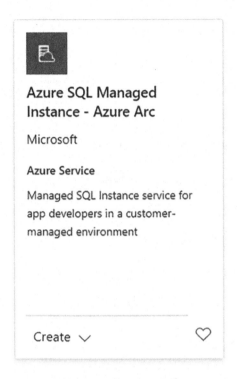

Figure 7-16. *Azure Portal – Create Azure SQL Managed Instance - Azure Arc*

And click "Create" on the subsequent screen (Figure 7-17).

Figure 7-17. *Azure Portal – Create Azure SQL Managed Instance - Azure Arc*

On the first screen, you will provide basic information like the subscription and resource group to be used but also the name of the instance and the custom location (Figure 7-18).

Create Azure SQL Managed Instance - Azure Arc ···
Microsoft

Basics   Tags   Review + create

Deploy an Azure Arc-enabled SQL Managed Instance in the Kubernetes environment of your choice. Learn more

Project details

Select the subscription to manage deployed resources and costs. Use resource groups like folders to organize and manage all your resources.

Subscription * ⓘ	Demo Subscription ⌄
└──── Resource group * ⓘ	arcBook ⌄

Managed Instance details

Instance name * ⓘ	mi-direct-1 ✓
Custom location * ⓘ	arc-direct (arc-direct) ⌄

> ⓘ You can only deploy to custom locations that you have access to and for which a data controller has been configured. Learn more.

Service type * ⓘ	NodePort ⌄
Compute + Storage ⓘ	**2 vCores, 4 Gi memory** Configure compute + storage

Figure 7-18. *Azure Portal – Create Azure SQL Managed Instance - Azure Arc – Basics*

On the Configure compute + storage page (Figure 7-19), you can not only define your Storage Classes, requests, and limits, but this is also where you'd pick the tier and therefore decide on the number of replicas. Based on these settings, you'll also be provided an estimated cost.

Configure compute + storage   ⋯

Service Tier

Select from the latest vCore service tiers available for SQL Managed Instance - Azure Arc including General Purpose and Business Critical. Learn more ◱

Service tier ⓘ

○ **General Purpose** (Up to 24 vCores and 128 Gi of RAM, standard high availability)

○ **[PREVIEW] Business Critical** (Unlimited vCores and RAM, advanced high availability)

For development use only ⓘ   ☐

High availability

Enable additional replicas for high availabilty. The compute and storage configuration selected below will be applied to all replicas.

High availability * ⓘ   ◉ 1 replica

Instance Compute

Configure compute utilization limits for your instance.

Memory Request (in Gi) *	2	✓
CPU vCores Request *	2	✓
Memory Limit (in Gi) *	4	✓
CPU vCores Limit *	2	✓

Instance Storage

Configure storage class and utilization limits for your instance data, logs and backups storage.

Data storage class	<default>

Cost summary

General Purpose

Cost per vCore (in USD)	153.00
CPU vCores Limit	x 2
Azure Hybrid Benefit discount (in USD)	- 0

ESTIMATED COST PER MONTH   **306.00** USD

Additional charge per usage
See pricing details for more detail.

Figure 7-19. *Azure Portal – Create Azure SQL Managed Instance - Azure Arc – Configure compute + storage*

The last information that you need to key in (see Figure 7-20) are the username and password for the admin account.

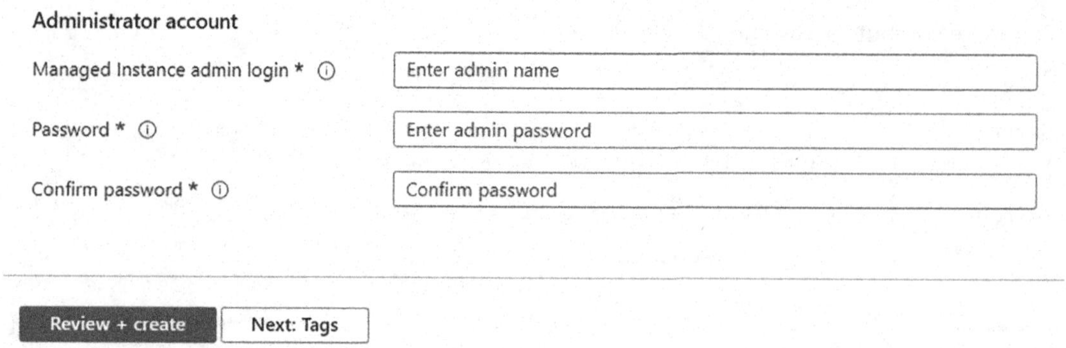

Administrator account

Managed Instance admin login * ⓘ

> Enter admin name

Password * ⓘ

> Enter admin password

Confirm password * ⓘ

> Confirm password

[Review + create]   [Next: Tags]

Figure 7-20. *Azure Portal – Create Azure SQL Managed Instance - Azure Arc – Administrator account*

Unless you want to provide any Azure tags for this instance, you can go straight to the Review + create screen and deploy your instance as shown in Figure 7-21.

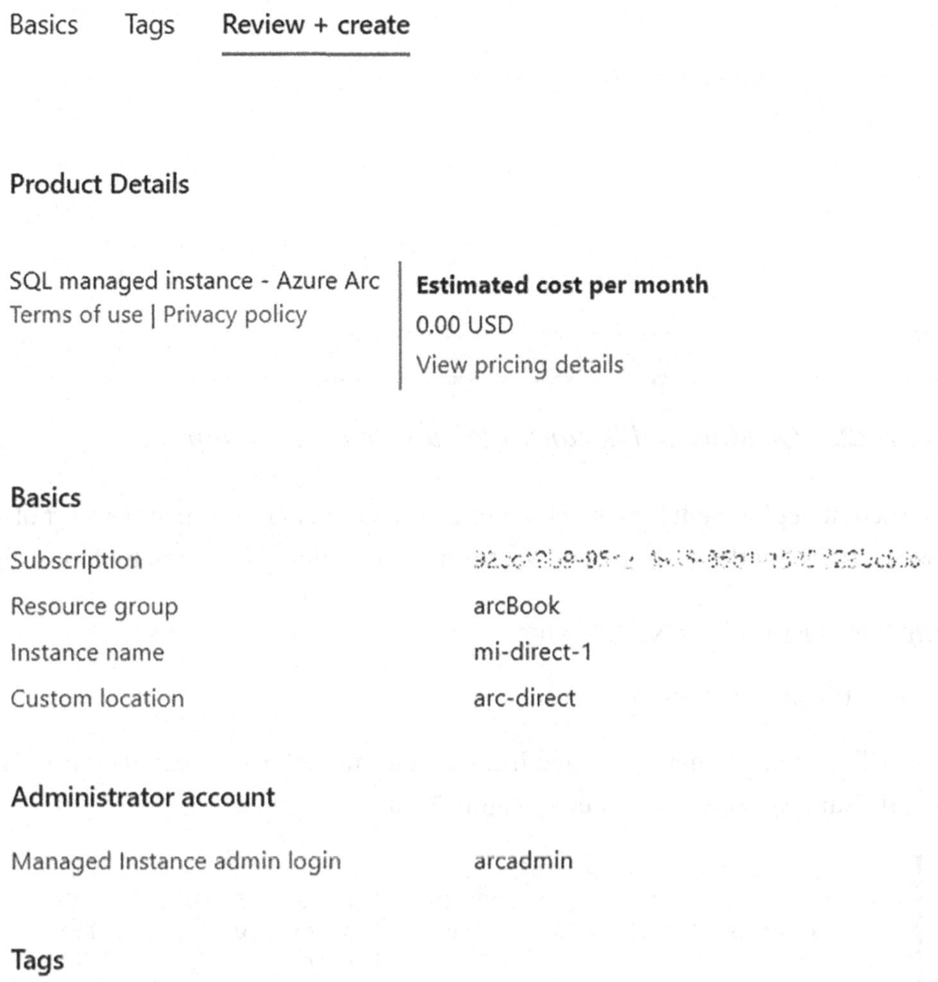

Basics   Tags   **Review + create**

Product Details

SQL managed instance - Azure Arc	**Estimated cost per month**
Terms of use | Privacy policy	0.00 USD
	View pricing details

Basics

Subscription	82c0*9L9-0%*2 *c*(%-86o*-*1%*f %*20c5.5
Resource group	arcBook
Instance name	mi-direct-1
Custom location	arc-direct

Administrator account

Managed Instance admin login	arcadmin

Tags

Figure 7-21. *Azure Portal – Create Azure SQL Managed Instance - Azure Arc – Review + create*

After deployment, the instance will show up in your resource group immediately (Figure 7-22).

Resources   Recommendations

| Filter for any field... | Type == **all** ✕ | Location == **all** ✕ | ⁺▽ Add filter |

Showing 1 to 5 of 5 records. ☐ Show hidden types ⓘ

☐ Name ↑↓	Type ↑↓
☐ 🗄 arc-dc-direct	Azure Arc data controller
☐ 🔧 arc-direct	Custom location
☐ 🔳 arcBookLAWS	Log Analytics workspace
☐ 🖥 kubeadm	Kubernetes - Azure Arc
☐ 🗄 mi-direct-1	SQL managed instance - Azure Arc

Figure 7-22. *SQL Managed Instance in Azure Resource Group*

The actual deployment however happened on our local Kubernetes Cluster of course, so check out the Pods in your Arc Namespace using the command in Listing 7-9.

Listing 7-9. List Pods in Namespace

```
kubectl get pods -n arc-direct
```

You will see that the new Managed Instance has indeed been created on this Cluster and in this Namespace as illustrated in Figure 7-23.

```
C:\>kubectl get pods -n arc-direct
NAME                               READY   STATUS    RESTARTS   AGE
bootstrapper-66c7779f5f-6tcmd      1/1     Running   0          17h
control-bvqv8                      2/2     Running   0          17h
controldb-0                        2/2     Running   0          17h
logsdb-0                           3/3     Running   0          17h
logsui-8b272                       3/3     Running   0          17h
metricsdb-0                        2/2     Running   0          17h
metricsdc-cg9zv                    2/2     Running   0          17h
metricsdc-dn2sx                    2/2     Running   0          17h
metricsdc-vsk5q                    2/2     Running   0          17h
metricsui-l6w6z                    2/2     Running   0          17h
mi-direct-1-0                      4/4     Running   0          2m48s
mi-direct-1-ha-0                   2/2     Running   0          2m48s
```

Figure 7-23. *Arc Pods in Kubernetes Namespace*

Active Directory Authentication

At the time of writing, Active Directory authentication was still in preview. You can find the most recent step-by-step guide in the official docs at *https://docs.microsoft.com/ en-us/azure/azure-arc/data/active-directory-introduction*.

Getting Data into Your Instance

If you want to restore an existing database in your instance, the first step in most cases is to copy this database's backup into your container – or rather onto the storage behind your container. Since Arc SQL Managed Instance is the lift-and-shift version of SQL Server, to get data into an Arc SQL Managed Instance, you can simply use a standard SQL Server backup.

Copying Backup Files into Your Instance

As so often, there are multiple ways of getting your backup files into your Arc SQL Managed Instance, and we'll again give you some options. If you have a backup file that can be downloaded using HTTP, you can use kubectl to trigger a download with *wget* in your container (see Listing 7-10).

Listing 7-10. Code to download a file using wget within a container

```
kubectl exec mi-1-0 -n arc -c arc-sqlmi -- wget https://github.
com/Microsoft/sql-server-samples/releases/download/adventureworks/
AdventureWorks2019.bak -O /var/opt/mssql/data/AdventureWorks2019.bak
```

If you have a local backup file, on the other hand, you can also use kubectl to copy this file to the container as shown in Listing 7-11.

Listing 7-11. Code to copy a local file to a container

```
kubectl cp c:\files\AdventureWorks2017.bak arc/arc-mi-01-0:var/opt/mssql/
data/AdventureWorks2017.bak -c arc-sqlmi
```

Both techniques lead to the backup file sitting in your container. Make sure that there is enough disk space in the container and delete the backup file when you're finished. It usually depends on where your backup is originally coming from to make a decision which way makes more sense for you.

Restoring Backup Files in Your Instance

If you want to restore from the command line, you could either use a tool like *sqlcmd* directly from your client or use kubectl once again to run sqlcmd directly on the SQL Instance as shown in Listing 7-12.

Listing 7-12. Code to run sqlcmd within a container to restore a database from backup

```
kubectl exec mi-1-0 -n arc -c arc-sqlmi -- /opt/mssql-tools/bin/
sqlcmd -S localhost -U arcadmin -P "P@ssw0rd" -Q "RESTORE DATABASE
[AdventureWorks2019] FROM  DISK = N'/var/opt/mssql/data/AdventureWorks2019.
bak' WITH  FILE = 1,  MOVE N'AdventureWorks2017' TO N'/var/opt/mssql/data/
AdventureWorks2019.mdf',  MOVE N'AdventureWorks2017_log' TO N'/var/opt/
mssql/data-log/AdventureWorks2019_log.ldf',  NOUNLOAD,  STATS = 5"
```

You could also connect to the instance in Azure Data Studio and use the restore wizard or any other tool that can connect to a SQL endpoint.

Note   When connecting to a SQL Server with a different port than the default, when copying the endpoint, make sure to use a comma rather than a colon to separate the IP address and the port.

One other option would of course also be to restore the database from an Azure Blob Storage using the RESTORE FROM URL command. What you could do in addition to that would be to add another Persistent Volume that can be an external share or a dedicated backup disk which especially makes sense for larger backup and restore operations without bloating the containers storage or having to copy backups around.

Managed Backup and Restore

Every Azure Arc-enabled SQL Managed Instance comes with a built-in automatic backup feature which is enabled by default. This means that every single database that gets created or restored will automatically receive an initial full backup followed by scheduled differential and transaction log backups. This concept is very similar to the managed backup in an Azure SQL Managed Instance and allows you to perform a point-in-time restore to any specific timestamp within your retention period.

A restore will always be performed into a new database.

At the time of writing, full backups are taken once a week, differential backups are taken every 12 hours, and transaction log backups every 5 minutes with these settings not being configurable.

While all backup settings can be found and controlled through both the azure-cli as well as native Kubernetes tools, the easiest way to get started is the backup section of the instance's settings in Azure Data Studio as shown in Figure 7-24.

Figure 7-24. *Backup settings*

From there, you can change the retention time (Figure 7-25) for point-in-time recovery backups from its default (7 days) to anything from 1 to 35 days. Backup files older than the configured retention period are automatically deleted.

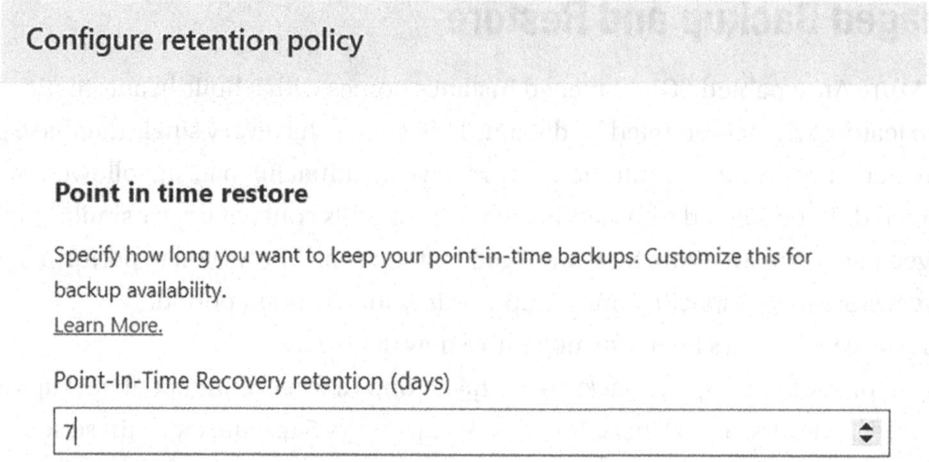

Configure retention policy

Point in time restore

Specify how long you want to keep your point-in-time backups. Customize this for backup availability.
Learn More.

Point-In-Time Recovery retention (days)

```
7
```

Figure 7-25. *Configure retention policy*

Changing the retention time to zero disables managed backups on this instance.

You could also adjust that setting by editing the instance's YAML manifest or by specifying the *--retention-days* property in the azure-cli.

You can also use Azure Data Studio or any of the other tools to trigger a restore (see Figure 7-26).

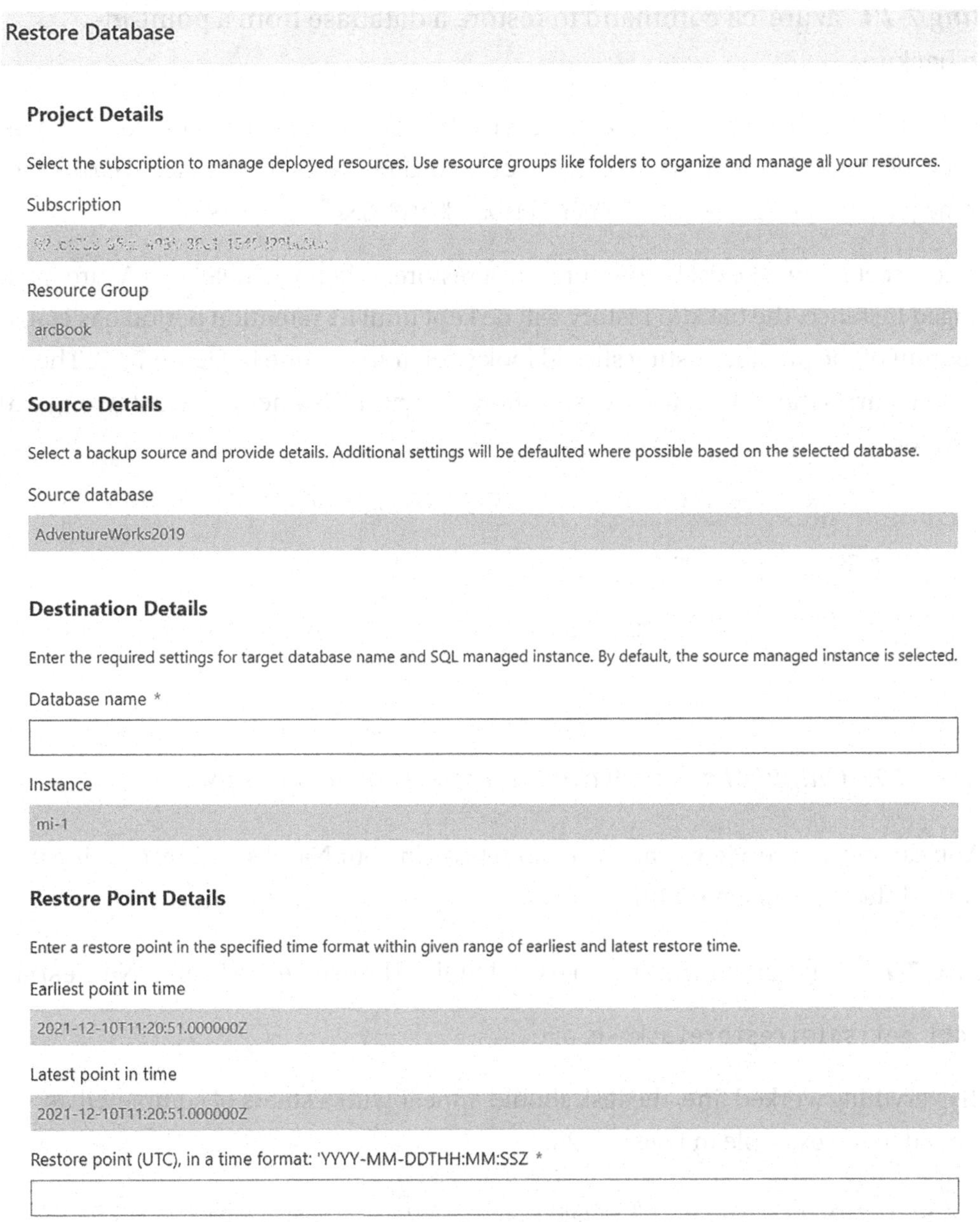

Restore Database

Project Details

Select the subscription to manage deployed resources. Use resource groups like folders to organize and manage all your resources.

Subscription

Resource Group

arcBook

Source Details

Select a backup source and provide details. Additional settings will be defaulted where possible based on the selected database.

Source database

AdventureWorks2019

Destination Details

Enter the required settings for target database name and SQL managed instance. By default, the source managed instance is selected.

Database name *

Instance

mi-1

Restore Point Details

Enter a restore point in the specified time format within given range of earliest and latest restore time.

Earliest point in time

2021-12-10T11:20:51.000000Z

Latest point in time

2021-12-10T11:20:51.000000Z

Restore point (UTC), in a time format: 'YYYY-MM-DDTHH:MM:SSZ *

Figure 7-26. *Restore Database in Azure Data Studio*

A restore requires a source database, destination database, and the restore point (timestamp).

Alternatively, you could, for example, also use the azure-cli and a command similar to the one in Listing 7-13 to restore your backup.

Listing 7-13. azure-cli command to restore a database from a point-in-time backup

```
az sql midb-arc restore --managed-instance <SQL managed instance> --name
<source DB name> --dest-name <Name for new db> --k8s-namespace <namespace
of managed instance> --time "YYYY-MM-DDTHH:MM:SSZ" --use-k8s
```

The target MI must exist before running a restore. When you delete an Azure Arc SQL Managed Instance, the backup history will be kept until its retention period has elapsed. The output of the previous listing should look similar to the one in Figure 7-27. The important part is the state. If this doesn't show *Completed*, something went wrong with your restore.

```
C:\>az sql midb-arc restore --managed-instance mi-1 --name AdventureWorks2019 --dest-name aw2019-restore --k8s-namespace
 arc --time 2021-12-10T11:27:19.000000Z --use-k8s
{
    "sourceDatabase": "AdventureWorks2019",
    "destDatabase": "aw2019-restore",
    "restorePoint": "2021-12-10T11:27:19.000000Z",
    "earliestRestoreTime": "0001-01-01T00:00:00.000000Z",
    "latestRestoreTime": "0001-01-01T00:00:00.000000Z",
    "message": "Restore operation completed successfully.",
    "observedGeneration": 1,
    "state": "Completed"
}
```

Figure 7-27. *Output of azure-cli command to restore a database*

You can get an overview of all the restore tasks in your Namespace by running the command shown in Listing 7-14.

Listing 7-14. kubectl command to list all SQL MI Restore Tasks in a Namespace

```
kubectl get sqlmirestoretask -n arc
```

If everything worked fine, the task should appear with a status of completed as illustrated in the example in Figure 7-28.

```
sql-restore-1639135964.498202   Completed   15s
```

Figure 7-28. *Status of a SQL MI Restore Task*

To retrieve more details, especially in the case of a failed restore task, you can use the command in Listing 7-15 to describe the task and analyze what made it fail.

Listing 7-15. kubectl command to describe a SQL MI Restore Task

```
kubectl describe sqlmirestoretask <nameoftask> -n <namespace>
```

Of course, the restored database also becomes visible in Azure Data Studio as visible in Figure 7-29.

Databases

Name	Status
master	Online
msdb	Online
tempdb	Online
AdventureWorks2019	Online
aw2019-restore	Online

Figure 7-29. *Restored Database showing up in Azure Data Studio*

A restore task could of course also be created through native Kubernetes tools just like you could also adjust settings like the retention policy from there.

Removing a Deployed Managed Instance

If you want to remove an existing deployed Managed Instance, you can do so through its management page in Azure Data Studio as shown in Figure 7-30.

Figure 7-30. *Delete button for an existing SQL MI in ADS*

Before the instance gets deleted, you will be prompted and asked to confirm by typing the name of the instance (see Figure 7-31).

Warning! Deleting an instance is permanent and cannot be undone. To delete the instance 'mi-4' type the name 'mi-4' below to proceed.

mi-4

Press 'Enter' to confirm your input or 'Escape' to cancel

Figure 7-31. *Confirmation dialog to delete an existing SQL MI in ADS*

Alternatively, you can use another az command as shown in Listing 7-16.

Listing 7-16. azure-cli command to delete an existing SQL MI

```
az sql mi-arc delete -n <InstanceName> -k arc --use-k8s
```

This will be confirmed shortly after with a message similar to the one in Figure 7-32.

```
C:\>az sql mi-arc delete -n mi-3-ads -k arc --use-k8s
Deleted mi-3-ads from namespace arc
```

Figure 7-32. *Output of delete command for an existing SQL MI*

Note   When deleting an instance through the CLI, there is no additional prompt or warning.

When deleting an instance, this will only remove its pods but not the storage (Persisted Volume Claims) that was used by the instance. To delete those as well, we must first identify the affected PVCs using kubectl as shown in Listing 7-17.

Listing 7-17. kubectl command to list the PVCs of an instance based on labels

```
kubectl get pvc -n <Namespace> -l <label> -o name
```

This will return a list of the PVCs used by this instance (see Figure 7-33). This naming scheme depends on the storage provisioner in use. The ones in our example came from the local storage provisioner, so yours may look different if you're using a different storage subsystem.

```
C:\>kubectl get pvc -n arc -l controller=mi-3-ads -o name
persistentvolumeclaim/backups-vz0d9494xj1lnrlmhjzx6njw-mi-3-ads-0
persistentvolumeclaim/data-ha-vz0d9494xj1lnrlmhjzx6njw-mi-3-ads-ha-0
persistentvolumeclaim/data-vz0d9494xj1lnrlmhjzx6njw-mi-3-ads-0
persistentvolumeclaim/datalogs-vz0d9494xj1lnrlmhjzx6njw-mi-3-ads-0
persistentvolumeclaim/logs-ha-vz0d9494xj1lnrlmhjzx6njw-mi-3-ads-ha-0
persistentvolumeclaim/logs-vz0d9494xj1lnrlmhjzx6njw-mi-3-ads-0
```

Figure 7-33. *List of PVCs of an instance*

Using the names of those PVCs, we can then use another kubectl command (see Listing 7-18) to delete them.

Listing 7-18. kubectl command to delete a PVC based on labels

```
kubectl delete pvc -n <Namespace> -l <label> -o name
```

This deletion will also be confirmed by kubectl, and when checking back for any remaining claims by this instance, we can tell from Figure 7-34 that none should be left.

```
C:\>kubectl delete pvc -n arc -l controller=mi-3-ads -o name
persistentvolumeclaim/backups-vz0d9494xj1lnrlmhjzx6njw-mi-3-ads-0
persistentvolumeclaim/data-ha-vz0d9494xj1lnrlmhjzx6njw-mi-3-ads-ha-0
persistentvolumeclaim/data-vz0d9494xj1lnrlmhjzx6njw-mi-3-ads-0
persistentvolumeclaim/datalogs-vz0d9494xj1lnrlmhjzx6njw-mi-3-ads-0
persistentvolumeclaim/logs-ha-vz0d9494xj1lnrlmhjzx6njw-mi-3-ads-ha-0
persistentvolumeclaim/logs-vz0d9494xj1lnrlmhjzx6njw-mi-3-ads-0

C:\>kubectl get pvc -n arc -l controller=mi-3-ads -o name

C:\>_
```

Figure 7-34. *Output of check if all PVCs have been deleted*

Summary and Key Takeaways

Over the course of this chapter, our ramp up building a Kubernetes Cluster and a Data Controller paid off as we were able to deploy and use our first actual Data Service in Arc using Azure Arc-enabled SQL Managed Instance.

In the next chapter, we'll take a look at how this process looks like when deploying an Azure Arc-enabled PostgreSQL Hyperscale instead.

CHAPTER 8

Deploying Azure Arc-enabled PostgreSQL Hyperscale

While Chapter 7 was handling Azure Arc-enabled SQL Managed Instance, this chapter will guide us through the necessary steps when it comes to working with PostgreSQL Hyperscale instead.

Deployment Through the Command Line

Just like an Azure Arc-enabled SQL Managed Instance, a new PostgreSQL Hyperscale Server Group can be deployed through a simple az command like the one in Listing 8-1. The only required parameter is the name of the Server Group.

Listing 8-1. azure-cli command to create a new PostgreSQL Hyperscale Server Group

```
az postgres arc-server create --name pg-1 --k8s-namespace arc --use-k8s
```

Note   The same logic as with SQL Managed Instance with regard to the use of direct vs. indirect mode and the --use-k8s switch applies here, too.

Still, you have full control of the deployment's settings through command-line switches if you prefer to do so, as in Listing 8-2.

149

© Ben Weissman and Anthony E. Nocentino 2022
B. Weissman and A. E. Nocentino, *Azure Arc-enabled Data Services Revealed*,
https://doi.org/10.1007/978-1-4842-8085-0_8

Listing 8-2. azure-cli command to create a new PostgreSQL Hyperscale Server Group with parameters

```
az postgres arc-server create --name pg-2 `
--k8s-namespace arc --use-k8s `
--storage-class-data local-storage `
--storage-class-logs local-storage `
--storage-class-backups local-storage `
--workers 4 --port 5432 --engine-version 12 `
--volume-size-data 5Gi --volume-size-logs 5Gi `
--volume-size-backups 5Gi
```

In either way, the azure-cli will prompt you for a password unless you provided it through the AZDATA_PASSWORD environment variable and then proceed with the deployment as shown in Figure 8-1. Every PostgreSQL Hyperscale Server Group has a default administrative account username called *postgres*, which is not configurable.

```
C:\>az postgres arc-server create --name pg-1 --k8s-namespace arc --use-k8s --storage-class-data local-storage --s
torage-class-logs local-storage --storage-class-backups local-storage -w 4 --port 5432 --engine-version 12 --volum
e-size-data 5Gi --volume-size-logs 5Gi --volume-size-backups 5Gi
Command group 'postgres arc-server' is in preview and under development. Reference and support levels: https://aka
.ms/CLI_refstatus
Postgres Server password:
Confirm Postgres Server password:
Deploying pg-1 in namespace `arc`
pg-1 is Ready
```

Figure 8-1. *Output of PostgreSQL Hyperscale Server Group deployment command*

Other than that, there is no difference compared to the deployment of a SQL Managed Instance.

The Control Node and the Worker Nodes show up as individual Pods using kubectl (see Figure 8-2). These Nodes are independent from the Kubernetes Nodes!

```
C:\>kubectl get pods -n arc | grep pg
pg-1c0-0           3/3      Running    0        2m
pg-1w0-0           3/3      Running    0        2m
pg-1w0-1           3/3      Running    0        2m
pg-1w0-2           3/3      Running    0        2m
pg-1w0-3           3/3      Running    0        2m
```

Figure 8-2. *Postgres Pods*

Deployment Through Azure Data Studio

Of course, deployment through Azure Data Studio is also an option again. In the wizard as shown in Figure 8-3, simply pick the PostgreSQL option instead.

Figure 8-3. *Instance deployment wizard in ADS*

The following screen will check for the prerequisites again, followed by (see Figure 8-4) collecting the PostgreSQL Hyperscale Server Group-specific settings. Just like when deploying our SQL Managed Instance before, we will need to provide a name for this PostgreSQL Hyperscale Server Group and a password. The username is defaulted to *postgres*, so this setting won't be required. A PostgreSQL Hyperscale Server Group requires you to provide the number of workers. It is defaulted to 0 which would deploy a one-Node PostgreSQL Hyperscale Server Group, the TCP Port, as well as your Storage Classes, storage sizes, and CPU and memory requests and limits. As we've mentioned in Chapter 1, these settings will define on how many resources this specific deployment will allocate on your Kubernetes Cluster.

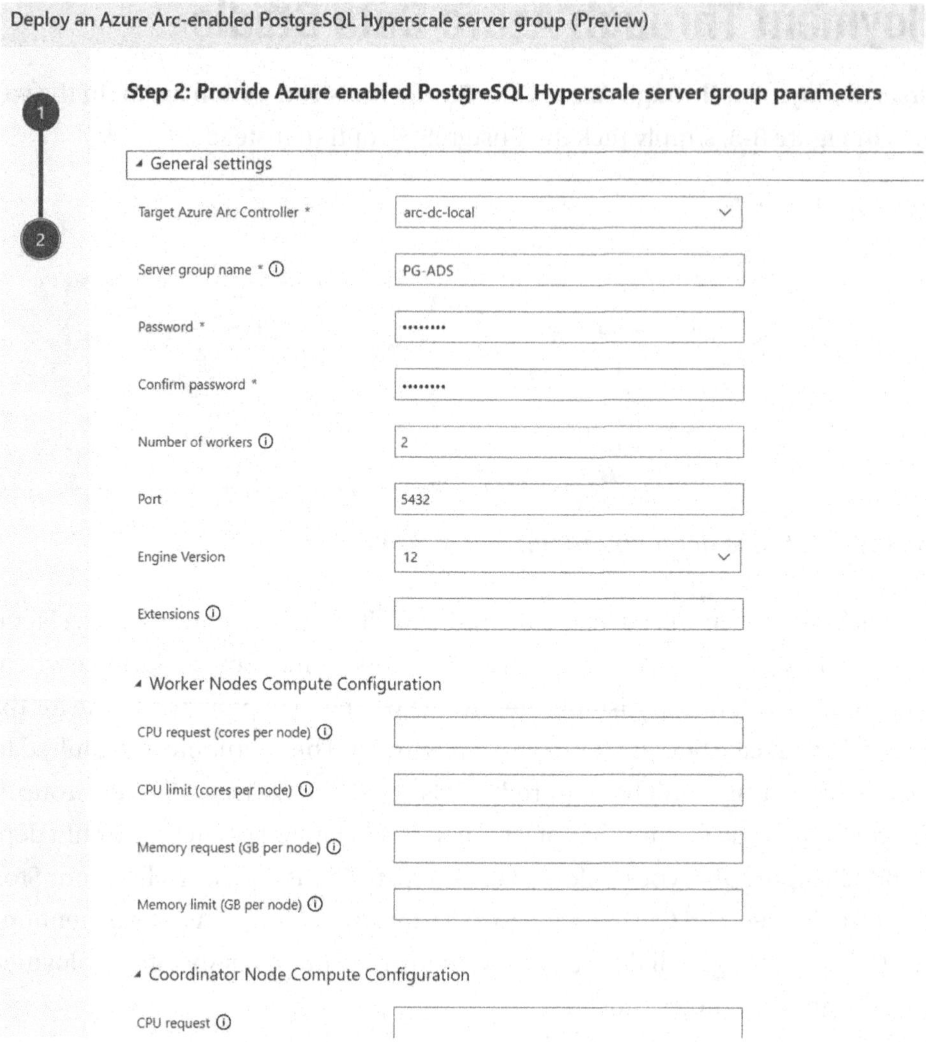

Deploy an Azure Arc-enabled PostgreSQL Hyperscale server group (Preview)

Step 2: Provide Azure enabled PostgreSQL Hyperscale server group parameters

◢ General settings

Target Azure Arc Controller *	arc-dc-local
Server group name * ⓘ	PG-ADS
Password *	••••••••
Confirm password *	••••••••
Number of workers ⓘ	2
Port	5432
Engine Version	12
Extensions ⓘ	

◢ Worker Nodes Compute Configuration

CPU request (cores per node) ⓘ	
CPU limit (cores per node) ⓘ	
Memory request (GB per node) ⓘ	
Memory limit (GB per node) ⓘ	

◢ Coordinator Node Compute Configuration

CPU request ⓘ	

Figure 8-4. Postgres-specific settings

This will result in the option of deploying this right away or to create a notebook which, when run, will create the new server group.

Scale Up of a Server Group

If you want to scale up an existing server group by adding more workers, this can be – you guessed it – achieved just by another small azure-cli command like the one in Listing 8-3.

Listing 8-3. azure-cli command to modify a server group's number of workers

```
az postgres arc-server edit --k8s-namespace arc --use-k8s -n pg-1 -w 8
```

This will update the existing server group while keeping it online, so the service remains available for queries. Once the Postgres Worker Nodes are available, the data will automatically be redistributed to these new Nodes by the Hyperscale Shard Rebalancer.

While an update is running, the affected server group will show as "Updating" in the server list (see Listing 8-4 and Figure 8-5).

Listing 8-4. azure-cli command to list all PostgreSQL Hyperscale Server Group in the current controller

```
az postgres arc-server list --k8s-namespace arc --use-k8s -o table
```

```
C:\>az postgres arc-server list --k8s-namespace arc --use-k8s -o table
Command group 'postgres arc-server' is in preview and under development.
I_refstatus
Name    Replicas    State     Workers
------  ----------  --------  ----------
pg-1    1           Updating  8
```

Figure 8-5. *List of PostgreSQL Hyperscale Server Group in the current Controller*

The edit command used to rescale the group will report back once the update has finished and the new workers are ready as shown in Figure 8-6.

```
C:\>az postgres arc-server edit --k8s-namespace arc --use-k8s -n pg-1 -w 8
Command group 'postgres arc-server' is in preview and under development. R
.ms/CLI_refstatus
Updating pg-1 in namespace `arc`
pg-1 is Ready
```

Figure 8-6. *Output of successful rescaling of a server group*

The new workers show up as individual Pods using kubectl (see Figure 8-7), besides the existing Control Node and Worker Nodes.

```
C:\>kubectl get pods -n arc | grep pg
pg-1c0-0              3/3        Running    0          3m42s
pg-1w0-0              3/3        Running    0          3m42s
pg-1w0-1              3/3        Running    0          3m41s
pg-1w0-2              3/3        Running    0          3m41s
pg-1w0-3              3/3        Running    0          3m41s
pg-1w0-4              3/3        Running    0          69s
pg-1w0-5              3/3        Running    0          69s
pg-1w0-6              3/3        Running    0          69s
pg-1w0-7              3/3        Running    0          69s
```

Figure 8-7. *Postgres Worker Pods*

The change is also reflected on the server group's management page in Azure Data Studio as shown in Figure 8-8. As you can see, this is also showing a Node configuration of five Nodes – which are again the Controller and the four Worker Nodes within our PostgreSQL Hyperscale Server Group.

Figure 8-8. *PostgreSQL Hyperscale Server Group Management page*

Note   The number of Worker Nodes can only be scaled up; you cannot scale down an existing group! For this, you'd need to deploy a new server group and back up/restore your data.

Removing a Deployed Server Group

To remove a deployed Postgres Server Group, you can use the az command shown in Listing 8-5.

Listing 8-5. azure-cli command to delete an existing PostgreSQL Hyperscale
Server Group

```
az postgres arc-server delete --k8s-namespace arc -n pg-1 --use-k8s
```

Alternatively, you can also delete the group from the group's dashboard in Azure
Data Studio as shown in Figure 8-9.

Figure 8-9. *Button to delete an existing PostgreSQL Hyperscale Server
Group in ADS*

Both ways can be used to delete an existing instance.

Note   Just like with our SQL Managed Instance, deleting the server group will not
delete its Persistent Volume Claims. You will need to delete these manually through
kubectl again once you're sure you won't need the data anymore.

Summary and Key Takeaways

So far, we went through the concepts and offerings of Azure Arc-enabled Data Services
and deployed different data instances to it. In our upcoming last chapter, we will look at
how to manage and monitor our services' performance, how to analyze its log files, and
how to upgrade them to a new version.

CHAPTER 9

Monitoring and Management

So far, we have covered the architecture of Azure Arc-enabled Data Services as well as the necessary steps to deploy them.

In this last chapter, we will focus how to monitor your Azure Arc-enabled Data Services by leveraging both local management services as well as Azure's management capabilities and also how to upgrade an existing installation.

Monitoring Through the Data Controller

One way of monitoring your Azure Arc-enabled Data Services is through two built-in dashboards: the Grafana and the Kibana Dashboard. Using the built-in dashboards is especially handy when you don't have a regular or stable connection allowing you to sync your telemetry data to the Azure Portal on a regular basis. As we've mentioned in Chapter 2, those will be deployed locally to your Kubernetes Cluster while deploying your Data Controller.

Retrieving Endpoints

To get the URLs for the dashboards, you need to get their endpoints. You can either get them through *az* using the command in Listing 9-1.

Listing 9-1. azure-cli command to retrieve a list of controller endpoints

```
az arcdata dc endpoint list -o table -k arc
```

157

© Ben Weissman and Anthony E. Nocentino 2022
B. Weissman and A. E. Nocentino, *Azure Arc-enabled Data Services Revealed*,
https://doi.org/10.1007/978-1-4842-8085-0_9

Alternatively, every single data instance's management page in Azure Data Studio will have a deep link to the instance's prefiltered dashboards as shown in Figure 9-1.

Figure 9-1. *Portal endpoints for an Arc SQL Managed Instance on its management page in ADS*

Metrics (Grafana Dashboard)

The Grafana Portal provides metrics and insights on the status of its instances. The credentials to log in to the Portal will be the same ones you also used to connect to your Cluster in Azure Data Studio.

The SQL Managed Instance metrics as shown in Figure 9-2 provide SQL Server-specific performance metrics, many of which DBA are already familiar with.

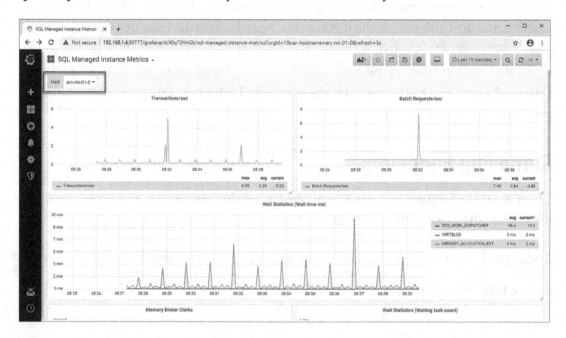

Figure 9-2. *Grafana Portal – SQL MI metrics*

Statistics show wait time, number of waiting tasks sorted by wait type, transactions and requests per second, and other valuable metrics. They help to understand more about the status of a specific SQL MI within the Cluster, which can be selected on the upper left of the screen.

The other dashboards currently available in the pre-configured Grafana Portal are shown in Figure 9-3.

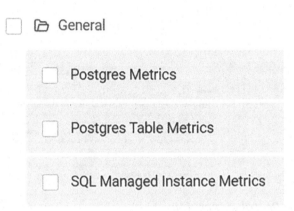

Figure 9-3. Built-in dashboards in Grafana Portal

Log Search Analytics (Kibana)

The Kibana Dashboard as shown in Figure 9-4, on the other hand, provides you an insight into your Kubernetes log files of the selected instance.

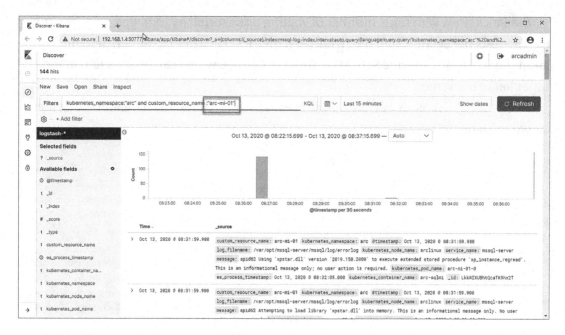

Figure 9-4. *Kibana Portal – overview*

Kibana is part of the elastic stack. It also provides options to create visualizations and dashboard on top of your log files. If you want to learn more about it, its website *www.elastic.co/products/kibana* is a great starting point!

Monitoring Through the Azure Portal

With one of the advantages of Arc being the opportunity to manage your whole estate through a single management interface, if your connectivity allows for it, we highly recommend linking your deployment to the Azure Portal. This is not going to take away the option to use Grafana and Kibana, so consider it a very valuable bonus.

Directly Connected Mode

When in directly connected mode, your log files and metrics will by default be automatically uploaded and synced to the Azure Portal.

Indirectly Connected Mode

In indirectly connected mode, you will first export your Cluster logs and metrics to a file and then upload this file on a regular basis. This process can also be scheduled and automated if needed to make sure your telemetry is regularly synchronized with the Azure Portal.

Preparing for Upload

The first requirement to run the upload is a service principal which you can create using the command in Listing 9-2.

Listing 9-2. azure-cli code to create a new service principal

```
az ad sp create-for-rbac --name http://arc-log-analytics
```

Note   The name of the service principal doesn't matter. We picked "arc-log-analytics" simply to make the name reflect its purpose.

Once your service principal has been created, you will get some JSON in return. You will need some of these values in the subsequent steps. The output should look similar to the one in Figure 9-5.

```
{
  "appId": "ab72c307-6c29-44c9-826f-0ae229d4e15b",
  "displayName": "arc-log-analytics",
  "name": "http://arc-log-analytics",
  "password": "Z5Q2n9SpEooBAHv81z9                ",
  "tenant": "314aef24-24ea-49b3-a6c6-a6a24b90949e"
}
```

Figure 9-5. Output of service principal creation

Next, we need to assign this new principal to the *Monitoring Metrics Publisher* role which can be done using the code in Listing 9-3. Make sure to replace the *appId* with the *appId value* from the previous JSON and the subscription with your *subscription ID*.

Listing 9-3. azure-cli code to assign a service principal to a role

```
az role assignment create --assignee <appId> --role "Monitoring Metrics
Publisher" --scope subscriptions/<Subscription>
```

This will result in a JSON output, similar to the one in Figure 9-6, again although none of this output is required later on.

```
{
  "canDelegate": null,
  "condition": null,
  "conditionVersion": null,
  "description": null,
  "id": "/subscriptions/                                    /providers/Microsoft.Authorization/roleAssignments/1ce5e773-41f4-4b84-8a36-0faf45d96354",
  "name": "1ce5e773-41f4-4b84-8a36-0faf45d96354",
  "principalId": "4ca6efad-e7de-44c7-9aaa-60a274c27898",
  "principalType": "ServicePrincipal",
  "roleDefinitionId": "/subscriptions/                                'providers/Microsoft.Authorization/roleDefinitions/3913510d-42f4-4e42-8a64-420
c390055eb",
  "scope": "/subscriptions/                                 ",
  "type": "Microsoft.Authorization/roleAssignments"
}
```

Figure 9-6. *Output of Listing 9-3*

In the next step, we create a Log Analytics Workspace using Listing 9-4.

Listing 9-4. azure-cli code to create a Log Analytics Workspace

```
az monitor log-analytics workspace create -g <ResourceGroup> -n
UniqueLogAnalytics
```

Note   Just like with the service principal, the name doesn't matter, but it must be globally unique. If you have deployed a Log Analytics Workspace during the deployment of the directly connected Data Controller, you can also reuse this one. While a Data Controller is either directly or indirectly connected, as many of them as you want can share the same Log Analytics Workspace.

This will again result in a JSON output (see Figure 9-7), and we will need the customerId value from this.

```
{
  "customerId": "e509e76d-9a42-49af-a11e-6a650dd0eeea",
  "eTag": null,
  "id": "/subscriptions/                              /resourcegroups/arcbook/providers/microsoft.operationalinsights/workspaces/arcbookloganalytics",
  "location": "eastus",
  "name": "arcBookLogAnalytics",
  "privateLinkScopedResources": null,
  "provisioningState": "Succeeded",
  "publicNetworkAccessForIngestion": "Enabled",
  "publicNetworkAccessForQuery": "Enabled",
  "resourceGroup": "arcbook",
  "retentionInDays": 30,
  "sku": {
    "capacityReservationLevel": null,
    "lastSkuUpdate": "Tue, 13 Oct 2020 08:54:27 GMT",
    "maxCapacityReservationLevel": 3000,
    "name": "pergb2018"
  },
  "tags": null,
  "type": "Microsoft.OperationalInsights/workspaces",
  "workspaceCapping": {
    "dailyQuotaGb": -1.0,
    "dataIngestionStatus": "RespectQuota",
    "quotaNextResetTime": "Wed, 14 Oct 2020 01:00:00 GMT"
  }
}
```

Figure 9-7. *Output of Listing 9-4*

In addition to the *customerId,* we will need the workspace's shared keys which are not included in the default output but can be retrieved through the command in Listing 9-5.

Listing 9-5. azure-cli code to retrieve a Log Analytics Workspace's shared keys

```
az monitor log-analytics workspace get-shared-keys
-g <ResourceGroup> -n UniqueLogAnalytics
```

This will return in a last JSON output as shown in Figure 9-8 from which we'll need the primarySharedKey.

```
{
  "primarySharedKey": "ZR5y2WSrrLMrulb5U05OIAnrxKT3zqixTANI83X2LRKvNCMhAb+aU3                    ",
  "secondarySharedKey": "S5zZxadL42WSQXapfCmOgr5b/e2k4YC6UgYdBZzTJSEYrWJ/BK1E                    =="
}
```

Figure 9-8. *Output of Listing 9-5*

Now, you should ideally put the results of some of these values into environment variables. You can skip this step but would then need to input them manually every single time which would make automation basically impossible. Those variables are

- SPN_CLIENT_ID: appId from the output of Listing 9-2
- SPN_CLIENT_SECRET: password from the output of Listing 9-2
- SPN_TENANT_ID: tenant from the output of Listing 9-2
- WORKSPACE_ID: customerId from the output of Listing 9-4

163

- WORKSPACE_SHARED_KEY: primarySharedKey from the output of
  Listing 9-5

- SPN_AUTHORITY: *https://login.microsoftonline.com*

Uploading Logs, Usage, and Metrics

As mentioned before, the process consists of two steps: first, we're going to collect the usage, logs, and metrics for every single deployment and write the result to a JSON file using the commands in Listing 9-6. The *--path* parameter will define the name of the output file, while the *--force* parameter will overwrite the target file in case it already exists.

Listing 9-6. azure-cli command to export metrics, usage, and logs to a json file

```
az arcdata dc export -t metrics --path metrics.json -k arc --force --use-k8s
az arcdata dc export -t logs --path logs.json -k arc --force --use-k8s
az arcdata dc export -t usage --path usage.json -k arc --force --use-k8s
```

az will confirm the export for each component as you can see in Figure 9-9.

```
C:\>az arcdata dc export -t metrics --path metrics.json -k arc --force --use-k8s
Upload status file: C:\Users\PSDemo\.azure\cliextensions\arcdata\arcdata-upload-status.json is saved.
Export custom resource: export-metrics-2021-12-10-12-22-06-1639138926810 is created.
Export custom resource: export-metrics-2021-12-10-12-22-06-1639138926810 state is Completed
```

Figure 9-9. *Output of Listing 9-6*

In the second step, we will upload these JSON files using the commands in Listing 9-7.

Listing 9-7. azure-cli command to upload metrics and logs from a json file

```
az arcdata dc upload --path metrics.json
az arcdata dc upload --path logs.json
az arcdata dc upload --path usage.json
```

In this case, *az* will confirm the upload for each component as you can see in Figure 9-10.

```
C:\>az arcdata dc upload --path metrics.json
        "arc-dc-local" is uploaded to Azure "/subscriptions/92cc49b9-95ca-4935-86e1-1545d29bc50a/resourcegroups/arcBook/
providers/Microsoft.AzureArcData/dataControllers/arc-dc-local"
        "mi-1" has been uploaded to Azure "/subscriptions/92cc49b9-95ca-4935-86e1-1545d29bc50a/resourcegroups/arcBook/pr
oviders/Microsoft.AzureArcData/sqlManagedInstances/mi-1".
        "mi-2" has been uploaded to Azure "/subscriptions/92cc49b9-95ca-4935-86e1-1545d29bc50a/resourcegroups/arcBook/pr
oviders/Microsoft.AzureArcData/sqlManagedInstances/mi-2".
        "arc-dc-local" is uploaded to Azure "/subscriptions/92cc49b9-95ca-4935-86e1-1545d29bc50a/resourcegroups/arcBook/
providers/Microsoft.AzureArcData/dataControllers/arc-dc-local"
Update status file metrics data_timestamp to 2021-12-10 12:22:06.000
```

Figure 9-10. *Output of Listing 9-7*

The upload is now completed. You could now go ahead, create a script file that combines the export and the upload, and schedule it to run on a regular basis, through cron, a windows scheduled task, or any other method of your choice to constantly get your insights pushed and made visible in the portal.

Monitor Your Resources in the Azure Portal

After uploading your logs and metrics for a resource for the first time, they can be found by searching in the Azure Portal (see Figure 9-11), side by side with the resources that were created in direct mode and therefore already showed up before.

Name ↑↓		Type ↑↓
☐	arc-dc-direct	Azure Arc data controller
☐	arc-dc-local	Azure Arc data controller
☐	arc-direct	Custom location
☐	arcBookLAWS	Log Analytics workspace
☐	kubeadm	Kubernetes - Azure Arc
☐	mi-1	SQL managed instance - Azure Arc
☐	mi-2	SQL managed instance - Azure Arc
☐	mi-direct-1	SQL managed instance - Azure Arc

Figure 9-11. *Arc Managed Instances showing in the Azure Portal*

Alternatively, every single data instance's dashboard in Azure Data Studio will have a deep link – just like when accessing the built-in dashboards – to the instance in the Azure Portal as shown in Figure 9-12.

≡ SQL managed instance - Azure Arc Dashboard (Preview) - arc-mi-01 ✕

« | 🗑 Delete ⟳ Refresh | ⬀ Open in Azure Portal

Figure 9-12. *Link to an Arc MI in the portal from ADS*

In the portal, you will again see the instance's details like which Data Controller is managing it as well as subpages for metrics and logs (see Figure 9-13).

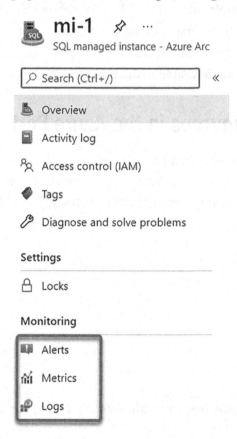

Figure 9-13. *Single Arc Managed Instance showing in the Azure Portal*

Note   Alerts only work for directly connected Clusters.

On the Metrics page, you can analyze the uploaded metrics, just like you could for an instance residing in Azure, as you can see in Figure 9-14.

Figure 9-14. *Arc SQL Managed Instance showing in the Azure Portal – Metrics*

The same logic applies to logs which can be analyzed using Log Analytics as shown in Figure 9-15.

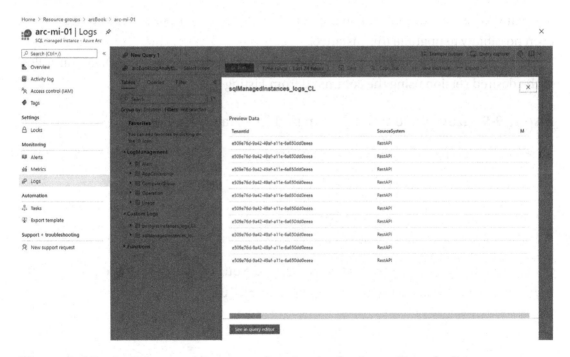

Figure 9-15. *Arc Managed Instance showing in the Azure Portal – Logs*

Upgrading Azure Arc-enabled Data Services

The first thing to check when you want to upgrade to a newer version of Arc-enabled Data Services is which version you are currently running and which versions would be available, which can be done using the code from Listing 9-8.

Listing 9-8. azure-cli command to list available upgrades for a Data Controller

```
az arcdata dc list-upgrades -k arc --use-k8s
```

The result will look similar to what we see in Figure 9-16.

```
C:\>az arcdata dc list-upgrades -k arc --use-k8s
Found 2 valid versions.  The current datacontroller version is v1.1.0_2021-11-02.
v1.1.0_2021-11-02 << current version
v1.0.0_2021-07-30
```

Figure 9-16. *Available upgrades for an Arc Data Controller*

In this case, our current version is already the latest version, so there is no need or even possibility to upgrade this instance.

However, if there would be, the process would be to first upgrade the Data Controller to the desired version using the command from Listing 9-9.

Listing 9-9. azure-cli command to upgrade a Data Controller

```
az arcdata dc upgrade [--desired-version]
                      [--dry-run]
                      [--k8s-namespace]
                      [--no-wait]
                      [--use-k8s]
```

Once your Data Controller has been upgraded, you could then upgrade your individual instances using the command in Listing 9-10.

Listing 9-10. azure-cli command to upgrade a SQL MI

```
az sql mi-arc upgrade --k8s-namespace
                      [--desired-version]
                      [--dry-run]
                      [--field-filter]
                      [--force]
                      [--label-filter]
                      [--name]
                      [--use-k8s]
```

Summary and Key Takeaways

In this last chapter, we've explored the options of getting an overview of your Azure Arc-enabled Data Services' status as well as how to link your deployment to the Azure Portal to make metrics and log files available for analysis. In our final step, we also checked out how Azure Arc-enabled Data Services can be upgraded.

Index

© Ben Weissman and Anthony E. Nocentino 2022
B. Weissman and A. E. Nocentino, *Azure Arc-enabled Data Services Revealed*,
https://doi.org/10.1007/978-1-4842-8085-0

N, O

Network Address Translation (NAT), 21

NodePort, 10, 11, 97, 123

P, Q, R

Persistent storage, 7, 9, 34

Persistent Volumes, 11, 83, 84

Platform as a Service (PaaS), 29, 66

Pod, 2–4, 6, 7

PostgreSQL Hyperscale

    Azure Data Studio, 151

    remove deployed server group,
        154, 155

scale up server

    group, 152–154

Server Group, 149, 150

S, T, U

Services, Kubernetes, 9–11

Static provisioning/dynamic
    provisioning, 12

V, W, X, Y, Z

Virtual machines (VMs), 28, 33, 65,
    66, 70, 72

Printed in the United States
by Baker & Taylor Publisher Services